PENGUIN BOOKS
A 256
THE SCOTS

MORAY McLAREN

THE SCOTS

MORAY McLAREN

PENGUIN BOOKS

HARMONDSWORTH · MIDDLESEX

FIRST PUBLISHED 1951

TO THE MEMORY OF
William Power

MADE AND PRINTED IN GREAT BRITAIN
FOR PENGUIN BOOKS LTD
BY T. AND A. CONSTABLE LTD

CONTENTS

INTRODUCTION

'MAN! You have a nerve.' These words, spoken in the cool Augustan beauty of the Signet Library in Edinburgh, spoken by that kindest and most scholarly of men, the Signet Librarian, spoken amidst the circumstance of thousands of tomes, books, pamphlets, and periodicals upon Scotland and Scottish history, learned, historical, frivolous, or ephemeral, did not deeply abash the present writer. They did not abash him because he had been saying them to himself ever since he had accepted the agreeable task of writing this book; and he well knew that they represented what would be the first thoughts of most of his fellow-countrymen who might learn of his attempts while he was making them. The half-quizzical, half-monitory, wholly Scottish words of the librarian standing at the centre of his empire of learning only put into sound for the first time what he knew would be a general comment as well as a private thought of his own – Man! he most certainly 'had a nerve'.

He was not abashed, moreover, because he knew that anyone, literally anyone who undertakes to write a book upon the Scots which shall in its intent be serious as well as popular, must 'have a nerve'. This is not because the story of the Scots and Scotland is subtle, difficult, full of difficulties, darknesses, and has been already largely written about (though it is all these things), but pre-eminently for another reason – the violently controversial nature of nearly every subject upon which he will be bound to touch.

We in Scotland are sometimes thought of as a hard-headed, practical people devoted only to the everyday affairs of the world about us. Even those, however, who do accept this glib and superficial judgement of us as a fact, are constantly being surprised by the readiness with which we all, even the most prosaic of us, lean upon our past, the eagerness with which we refer to it and the passion with which we disagree about it. The English who, though they are our nearest neighbours, are in many respects more different from us than are those geographically more distant, are the most surprised by this trait in us. They readily admit that we are, above everything else, a country of individuals and therefore prone to disputatiousness. But why dispute about the past? What is the good of it?

It would indeed be difficult to give a satisfactory answer to these questions. One can only say that we are a small family in the congregation of Europe, a family that has for a millennium struggled with varying success to establish and preserve its corporate, as well as what might be described as its individual, individuality. Such families as struggle on, both in success and in reverse, tend with age to develop a pride which is sometimes ridiculous, sometimes petty, sometimes worthy, self-sacrificing, noble, and touching; but, whatever be its quality, it relies much upon the past. And, family pride being what it is, the family may present a common face to the outside world, but within is full of disagreement about that past. It may readily be understood, then, that anyone who, in the middle of the twentieth century, writes about the Scots, must constantly refer to the past and in each reference must lay himself open to flat disagreement from many of his compatriots and close friends. He must indeed 'have a nerve'.

At the risk of labouring this point it must be stressed here that there can be few, if any, of the small countries of Europe whose past offers so rich a field for disagreement as does Scotland's. A cursory glance at a thousand years of our history will confirm this. There is no major event in it, and very few truly great figures which you can mention in a company of Scots without splitting them into two or more parties. It would be tedious and anticipatory to give a list of them here. Let the non-Scot who has any knowledge of our country reflect but for a moment on a few well-known personalities, places, and events – John Knox, Mary Stuart, the Reformation, the Wars of the Covenant, the Union of the English and Scottish Parliaments in 1707, the Rising of 1745, the Clan Campbell, the Highland clearances, the Industrial Revolution, the 'red Clyde', modern Edinburgh. He will know that but to name one of these in Scottish company is to set loose a spate of argument upon which he may be borne, silent and unresisting, for as long as he feels inclined to allow it. He would be mistaken, however, if he supposes that it is only these famous and controversial eminences in our story that can arouse controversy. He would be surprised if he could hear what we can do with figures, institutions, and events that he had supposed were accepted by all Scots with one mind – were, indeed, almost sacrosanct to us.

It would be unfair, however, to leave the impression from this that we are a cantankerous race whose main intellectual pleasure lies in disagreement. This is very far from true. The Scot, in his attitude towards his own past, is animated less by the spirit of opposition than by loyalties to ideas and persons with whom he feels personally connected. It is only by perceiving this strong personal element in the Scots attitude to the past that one can understand his deep feeling about it. The past is not a dead thing — it is something which has made him and lives in him and in his circumstances, his family and his country, which, as has been said before, is itself very much like a large family containing familiar virtues and familiar failings.

He who speaks for the family to the outside world, then, is always aware of the fact that, if he is to be honest and truthful with himself as well as (he hopes) readable by the public he is addressing, he will contradict the loyalties and sentiments of many other members of the family. This is inescapable. The reader, therefore, is entreated to remember that any statement in this book that passes beyond the most obviously verifiable fact, that hints even at the vaguest opinion on a matter of fact, is at once open to flat contradiction by others of the writer's compatriots. This, of course, particularly applies to those parts that deal with the interpretation of modern Scotland. It applies even to the ensuing chapter which is intended to be no more than the barest skeleton of Scottish history.

CHAPTER ONE

THE BARE BONES OF SCOTTISH HISTORY

THE country of Scotland takes its name from Irish invaders and settlers called the Scots, who came to the
northern end of Britain and its Western Isles in the fourth,
fifth, and sixth centuries. These incomers, as far as ruling
and, in the modern sense of the term, occupying Scotland, certainly took the place of the mysterious Picts who,
in a tribal fashion, had existed incoherently in all parts of
what we now call Scotland for centuries. That the Celts
overcame the Picts there is no doubt, but it is not true, as
is sometimes stated, to say that they obliterated the older
race. The Picts were a tough people, and, to judge from
what remains of their stone carvings, gifted. It is likely
that they still, in blood, form the basis of the North-Eastern
Scottish type with its dourness and its independence.
Having supplanted the Picts the Irish Scots proceeded to
overcome, control, and absorb into their rule the Saxons
who had from the South invaded the Eastern portions of
what they looked upon as their territory. They succeeded
in doing this as far as the River Tweed, thus roughly, and
for the first time (if we discount the Roman Wall) estab-
lishing the border line between modern Scotland and
England, in 1018. The present definitions of the country
of Scotland are therefore about a millennium old; but the
birth of the nation may be placed earlier, when in 844
Kenneth Macalpine ascended the throne of the Picts

and the Scots and began the drive towards the present border.

The incoming Scots, amongst whom was St Columba, introduced, or at least disseminated, Christianity in the country they were to inhabit. They also brought with them the Gaelic tongue. This highly expressive, highly formal, and highly poetic language survives in the Western Highlands and may even be said to flourish in some of the islands. It is the oldest living language in Scotland, and is amongst the oldest in Europe.

It is characteristic of the enthusiastic veneration in which the Gaelic speakers hold their ancient speech that some of them describe it as 'the language talked by Adam and Eve in the Garden of Eden'.

Despite ferocious inroads made by the Norsemen who succeeded not only in spilling but strongly impregnating the blood of Celtic Scotland, despite continued attacks from the Saxons, Britons, and Angles in the South, the Gaelic Kingdom and the Gaelic way of life in Scotland remained established until the end of the eleventh century. Its first and most potent enemy arose within and at the very heart of it, in the person of the saintly Queen Margaret, wife of King Malcolm Canmore. This pious and vigorous Saxon Princess, who had almost by accident come into Scotland from England, set herself to reform the Celtic Church, to combat what seemed to her its outlandish, provincial, and casual customs. To do this she introduced Southern and Saxon clerics as well as Southern and Saxon ways in secular matters. Her vigour and piety were such that before her death the Celtic language and Celtic ways in the South of Scotland were becoming unfashionable amongst the ruling classes. The centuries-old subtle and weakening attack on Gaelic had begun. It was an attack which lasted until a time within living memory.

The father of the present writer, when a student at Edinburgh University, could remember lads from the Highlands who pretended that they did not speak Gaelic, so fearful were they that the polite world of Edinburgh would despise them for it. To-day, when the polite worlds of learning and of the arts positively cultivate Gaelic speech and music, such a state of affairs would be impossible. It is a question, however, whether the work which St Margaret began with such well-intentioned feminine and reforming zeal has not been too well done for its effects to be permanently checked. It is perhaps characteristic of the Gaels that they should have proved vulnerable to a thrust from such a quarter. Your Highlander can fight anyone but a woman.

The anglicization, if one may employ so loose a word for the combined Saxon and Norman influences upon Scotland that ensued, did not immediately have any effect upon the sense of nationality of the still comparatively young Kingdom of Scotland. It is possible, however, that had the peaceful penetration of Southern ideas begun by Margaret been allowed to continue, they might have had a political as well as a cultural and religious effect. But this was not to be. The English King Edward I, impelled by the ambition to unite and rule over all the island of Britain, and drawn on by his awareness of the increasing Norman influence in Scotland, launched his great and all but obliterating attack on the Northern Kingdom. Edward has been called 'the Hammer of the Scots'. It is a title to which time has given something of a double meaning. He may have hammered us so that we were nearly smashed, but in the end he hammered our nation into a hard fact.

The story of Scotland's struggle for independence against the fearful might of Edward I and England, and eventually and triumphantly against his son Edward II, need not here be sketched even in broad outlines. It is sufficient, in the schoolboy phrase, to say 'We won'. One may, however, pause to consider the two heroes who made our victory possible. They were two men united in purpose and in action, yet different in quality, two men whose separate characters are often reflected in the dichotomy of the Scotland that was to come centuries after them, the Scotland of to-day.

William Wallace is especially remarkable in that his resistance sprang into being at the most hopeless period of Scotland's prostration and in the fact that he, like the movement he inspired and led, emerged mysteriously and from obscurity. Though he was a Norman, his origin was humble; and he was known as 'the kinless loon'. He is perhaps a little obscure still; for he was a selfless and single-minded patriot untainted by ambition, and the very rarity of that quality makes him seem legendary to us to-day. His qualities would indeed have made him legendary at any time. Legendary he may be, but he is a legend for which Scotland feels profoundly and personally. This may spring partly from admiration for his bravery and for his achievements, and partly from the memory of his butchery at the hands of the English at Westminster – a memory grimly perpetuated in the name of Scotland Yard where the patriot was hanged, drawn, and quartered. But there is also another reason why the people of Scotland feel personally for him. He was one of them. He came from the heart of them, and has been enshrined in their hearts ever since.

Robert Bruce had larger and more resounding victories

in uniting Scotland and in the end defeating the English at Bannockburn. He was a different kind of man. He was as fearless as Wallace and as implacable; and on his achievements rests the basis of the Scotland that he freed. He was the hero of his day; but he is not quite such a hero in the warm, personal, though legendary sense that Wallace is for us in the posterity of Scotland. He was calculating, ruthless, and not without personal ambition; he came from the ruling class. We know much more what kind of man he was.

Still, he was a hero: and it is on the heroism of these two differing men that there was built the nation that for centuries after Bannockburn was to exist upon the fringes of Europe, proud, independent, and yet radically European. It is the nation which those of us who call ourselves Scotsmen still look upon as our Mother. Still our Mother, even if some of us may feel that the bountiful gift of her maternity has been squandered or bargained away by some of those who came after, centuries after Wallace and Bruce.

The victory in the Scottish wars of independence left Scotland, as victory so often does leave the victorious, jubilant yet weakened. The nation was now not only founded but established and recognized as such throughout Europe: it was, however, convalescent from its great struggle against death. Convalescence is the period when endemic failings discover themselves. And throughout the reigns of the Stewarts which, after a short interval, ensued upon the establishment of Scottish freedom, the most constant of all Scotland's constitutional ills (internal disunity, the fighting between men in high places) preyed unremittingly upon the body politic. This national evil was encouraged by the accident that nearly all of our monarchs of the fateful House of Stewart who were to rule over Scotland for two hundred years succeeded either in exile or in a period of minority.

The Stewarts (after Queen Mary spelled Stuart) were described by Voltaire as the most unfortunate Royal House in Europe. And, indeed, when one reflects upon the endings of these gifted, attractive, and often well-intentioned men and women from James I of Scotland to Prince Charles Edward Stuart, grandson of James VII of Scotland and II of England, one cannot but agree. Sudden death by the assassin or upon the battlefield or the execution block, or exile in disappointment and near despair, was the fate of all but two of the eleven heads of the house; and of those two, one, Charles II, had seen his father die by the axe and had spent the first years of his reign a wanderer in exile.

The time of this sad but remarkable procession of Kings and one Queen to the throne of Scotland and to the grave had more meaning for the country than providing her with the romantic story of a fated ruling family. It was in the era of the Stewarts, despite internal conflicts in high places, that Scotland, now comparatively sure of her position, began to develop something of the arts of peace. It was in these years that three of the four Scottish Universities were founded, that the 'Auld Alliance' with France, originating during the struggle for independence as a political manoeuvre, bore fruit in the encouragement of Scottish learning, in the establishment of that European and Continental strain in the Scottish character which distinguishes it in Great Britain even to-day. This Continental connexion was at this same time strengthened by the trade which grew up with the Low Countries and the habit then formed by

Scottish students of continuing their studies in Europe, notably at the Universities of Leyden and Bologna. It was under the greatest and most gifted of the Scottish Stewart Kings, James IV, that there dawned that brief morning of the Scottish Renaissance when at the Court in Holyrood poets were as important as politicians and musicians as ministers. It was a morning that was preternaturally thrust into the twilight when James and the flower of Scottish chivalry fell on the battlefield at Flodden, but it was a morning the effulgence of whose pristine rays still faintly illuminate our Scottish scene. It was when the last two Stewarts were reigning at Holyrood that there took place in Scotland that most momentous of all our social and intellectual movements – the Reformation.

The Reformation is the great watershed that divides, almost exactly in two, the millennium of Scotland's story. We who live upon the hither side of it can comprehend, even if we cannot sympathize with, everything that happened in Scotland after the Reformation; its effect is still so vivid that it touches us in every day of our daily life. Modern Scotland may be far from being entirely Presbyterian, Protestant, or even entirely Christian, but it is a Scotland which was fashioned and is still shaped by the Protestant Reformation and the Presbyterian Kirk. We who live in the valley of post-Reformation Scotland can see, after a fashion, everything in that valley. We have to learn at second hand to draw upon our imagination, to know what went on in the other valley of Catholic Scotland from which we are separated by the watershed.

It would be improper in this brief précis of a chapter to attempt any compressed account of this tremendous happening. Let it be enough here to say that by the Reformation Scotland achieved an even greater degree of independence, verging upon isolation. Not only did she sever herself from Rome, but she also put between herself and England the further barrier of a different faith. For though England underwent a Reformation at about the same time, hers was much more of a compromise; and the gulf between the Scottish Kirk and the Church of England was, in the eyes of her adherents, almost as great as that which divided her from Rome. This subject will be dealt with at a more suitable length in a later chapter.

In 1603 another event took place which, though it sprang from a mere accident of lineage, was of immense importance to Scotland – the Union of the Crowns under James VI of Scotland and I of England. When the Court left Holyrood for London, a unifying factor, however weak and ineffective it had often been, was removed from a country already prone to disunity. It is arguable that the religious wars and the fightings amongst the nobles which absorbed the energies of Scotland in the seventeenth century would not have been so severe had the Scottish Kings been in Scotland to act in some degree as a central authority. In this dark and savage century the figure of James Graham, Marquis of Montrose, Presbyterian Cavalier, soldier poet, shines like a lonely beacon. With Wallace, he is remarkable as being almost the only great figure of action in our past which in the process of time has passed nearly beyond controversy – controversy, that is, as to his quality and nature. He combined in himself nearly every strain in the Scottish character that is admirable.

The eighteenth century, in some ways the most remarkable in Scottish history, is especially remarkable for four things – the Union of the Scottish and English Parliaments, the extinction of the Gaelic way of life as an

18

independent unit in Scotland after the failure of the Jacobite Rising of 1745, the rise of modern Edinburgh and Glasgow, and, related to that last event, the Agricultural and Industrial Revolution, which raised Scotland from poverty to wealth within a few decades. Though it is perhaps more accurate to place the full force of the Industrial Revolution as taking place in the ensuing century.

The first of these events took place in 1707. It is regarded by some as the inevitable culmination of a beneficent tendency, the drawing together of England and Scotland, the unification of this island under one Government. Others, to put it mildly, do not take so kindly a view of this surrender of the ancient rights of the Scottish Parliament and the 'end of an auld sang'. They would still claim that that song is not ended and that the notes of its essential melody are even now to be heard.

The second event, the death-blow against the Highland way of life, is inseparably connected with the Jacobite Rising, 'the '45'. This celebrated and final attempt of Prince Charles Edward Stuart to regain the crown for his house has been the subject of so much romantic writing, both true and tinsel, and of such violent reaction against that romance that its true historical importance is often obscured. The question as to whether the subsequent history of the United Kingdom would have been profoundly affected had the Prince succeeded can be endlessly debated. One thing is certain: his failure was of immense importance to one half of Scotland. With the suppression of the old Highland feudal system of justice, with the forbidding of the Highland dress and the right of Highlanders to carry arms and, most of all, with the evictions of the Highland people, the old Gaelic dream of a Gaelic Scotland was finished. It truly was the 'end of an

19

auld sang'. Queen Margaret's work begun seven centuries earlier was completed.

The rise of Glasgow and the renaissance of Edinburgh in the second half of the eighteenth century laid the foundations of the modern Scotland – the Northern half of the United Kingdom. Glasgow's elevation or growth or wild and undisciplined expansion (again as you will) from being a quiet little University town on the banks of the Clyde to becoming the 'second city of the Empire' was due to the fact that the Union of the Parliaments allowed Scotland direct trade with the Americas and so opened the gateway of the Clyde to the Western world.

Edinburgh's astonishing recrudescence from about 1750 until the first two decades of the nineteenth century cannot be so easily accounted for. It is true that after the failure of the '45 in Great Britain, and the Northern Kingdom in particular, there was a general promise of peaceful and fairly prosperous times ahead. But that alone cannot explain the fact that Edinburgh, still small, black, crowded, and high perched upon a windswept Northern rock, became within fifty years the intellectual Capital of Great Britain and a lighthouse of European learning, whose gleams were visible upon the shores of the Mediterranean and beyond the frontiers of the Russias. The prospect of peace could not alone be responsible for David Hume, Adam Smith, Raeburn, Dugald Stewart, Walter Scott, and many other names internationally famous in their day, all rooted in Edinburgh. It is more likely that there occurred in the later half of the eighteenth century in Edinburgh and in Southern Scotland generally, despite many contrary factors, and because of some hidden spring within, one of these National revivals which are as incalculable as they are impressive.

The outward and visible sign of this remarkable Edinburgh period is still to be seen in the gracious and ordered beauty of the New Town, conceived if not entirely built by the civic renaissance of the late eighteenth-century Capital of Scotland.

In the nineteenth century the glory of Edinburgh, save for a certain amount of critical writing and famous medical research, declined into a pompous and torpid conservatism. And it was during these years that she acquired the supposedly odious reputation of being 'East Windy and West Endy'. Glasgow, on the other hand, continued to flourish, though less by the preaching of the word (as her civic motto proclaims) than by the exuberant if ruthless prosecution of modern industrial methods.

This was the century when the Industrial Revolution came to its fruition, the century of Scottish industry, apparent Scottish prosperity, and the inevitable concomitant of Scottish radicalism. To the Englishman, and to the inhabitant of the growing Megalopolis of London, it might well have seemed that never had Scottish individuality as a nation and in individual concerns and individual ideas so strongly proclaimed itself. In point of fact, this loud and sometimes strident publication of herself was Scotland's way of recompense for the loss of her individuality as a nation which she now began to feel though not to admit. Of course there were excellent and characteristically Scottish things that the people of Scotland achieved at this time – the founding of the Free Kirk, for instance, an epic of sacrifice to an ideal which was well worthy of the descendants of Scotsmen who had lived two centuries earlier. But in general a feeling began to be disseminated in Scotland which was felt much more strongly than it had been in the previous century when her Parliament had actually been surrendered, that Scotland was losing herself in Great Britain. It was this that made Scotsmen in the days of our grandfathers so often and so insistently proclaim their nationality, to the embarrassment of their friends and the tolerant amusement of foreigners.

Thus dawned the present century and the present age for Scotland. A Scotsman in 1900 who could have foreseen in a general form the content of the coming fifty years, with their world-wide tumults and disasters, their reckless obliteration of the age-old conv ntion of distance by modern scientific invention, and who could have above all else perceived the deep sickness of our Europe of to-day might well have shaken his head over the prospect of survival for his own country. 'This', he might have said to himself, 'will indeed be the end of an auld sang. This will be the finish of Scotland. How can this small country which has already lost the control of its own affairs, which has been partly absorbed by its powerful neighbour, which exists upon the fringe of a Europe already shrunk and ravaged, survive? It cannot.' But he would have been mistaken.

If he had not been mistaken, this book would not have been worth writing, for there would have been no object in chronicling, while it was going on, the ultimate decadence of a small unit of diverse but unified Europe. In the ensuing chapters an attempt will be made to present a picture of the Scots people in the modern Scotland that has so strangely, almost miraculously, survived a thousand years of attacks from without and distress and decay within – which has not only survived, but which looks forward to a new and still vigorous life. This present chapter in which those thousand years of

Scotland's story have been painfully compressed, is not only a background to the more immediate picture; it is something to which the reader will be from time to time referred as the present story is told. No people can be understood without reference to its past – least of all the Scots who are themselves so deeply conscious of their past.

CHAPTER TWO

THE GREAT DIVISION

1. *The Highlands and the Highlanders*

WHEN the young Scot goes for the first time into England or even further abroad, he often finds to his surprise that he is supposed to conform at different times and in different company to one of two highly opponent conceptions of 'the typical Scot'. Some of his new-found friends will expect him to be dour, unimaginative, cautious, reliable, and, if not exactly dull, good company only in a dry sardonic fashion, a master of understatement and in his general character to be compounded of the austere grey colours of the North. He will receive much good-humoured badinage when any of these supposed characteristics supposedly appear in him, and much surprise will be expressed when contrary qualities discover themselves.

With others of his companions he will find himself cast for a very different *rôle*. He will be expected to be high-spirited, gay, and melancholy by turns, something of a savage and something of a poet; and any moments of quietness or abstraction in his behaviour will be put down to a touch of 'feyness'. He is visualized at home as being draped in tartan and existing against a background of great natural beauty or in an eternal mist. The one characteristic which he is allowed in common by these two opposing views of him is an inordinate love of whisky.

Absurdly exaggerated though these caricatures of the Scottish character may be, your voyaging Scot who knows his own country must admit that there is a basis of fact for them. Moreover, if he is honest, he will admit that the reason for their existence is partly the kind of publicity that we have allowed and even encouraged to be put out about ourselves for the last two hundred years. Partly for purely practical and economic reasons, partly because it was held to be humorously effective, the notion of the dour, cautious, dry Scot has been exported from this country from the middle of the eighteenth century onwards. Partly as a reaction against this, and partly because it, too, was a selling proposition, the other and highly coloured conception of us has been much in favour ever since the romantic movement – that is ever since the failure of our last romantically conceived Rising in 1745 made it quite safe to romanticize us. Still, these two sides exist in our national character. If they had not, writers of the genius of Walter Scott and R. L. Stevenson would never have propagated the idea of them with such vigour and realism. Roughly speaking, the dry and cautious element in our character is Lowland and the more picturesque is Highland.

For a number of centuries until the Rising of 1745, this division of Scotland had been a very real thing. It was real in geography and real in the national character. Ever since Queen Margaret, a thousand years ago, began the attack on the Gaelic way of life, the Gaels had been retreating more and more into the then inaccessible mountain parts of Scotland. And by the fifteenth century they established themselves on the other side of the Highland line where they remained, preserving their language, their customs, their feudal methods of law-giving and, in many parts, their traditional Catholic faith against the Reformation in the South. The Highland line is not, as is sometimes supposed, a division between the North and the South. It runs from the north-east in Ross-shire and Sutherland south-west across Scotland to the verge of Glasgow and even, in some places, stretching south and west of Glasgow, as in the island of Arran.

The reality, the alarming reality of this Highland frontier line to our Lowland forefathers even as late as the early eighteenth century, is admirably set forth in Scott's *Rob Roy*. The Glasgow merchant Bailie Nicol Jarvie's unforgettable description of the wild old way of life that existed beyond the louring mountains as he took Francis Osbaldistone North from Glasgow is not only a superb piece of literature, it is an authentic historical cry from the not very remote past. It would be difficult to find a Scot with any feeling for his country who could read it without being moved and excited.

And here it is worth making a parenthetical and, from the structure of this book, a slightly anticipatory point. It is worth noting that a part of the Lowland Glasgow Bailie's gusto in describing the romantic terrors that lay beyond the Highland line came from the fact that in a remote (but characteristically carefully preserved) way, he was connected by blood with the most lawless of the Highland caterans – Rob Roy himself. To observe this is not only to pay tribute to Scott's literary and imaginative artistry but to recognize a cardinal fact about the old Highlanders and Lowlanders. Separated by the difference between mountain and plain, by difference in language and temperament, there was a frequently expressed sense of common nationality between the two. Sometimes this was discovered in the ties of blood, in the Scottish fashion long remembered and tenuously stretched. Sometimes it came to the surface when both Lowlander and Highlander were under the same pressure from without or found themselves as Scots together in a foreign country. Walter Scott's immortal Bailie was speaking not only for himself but for many of his Lowland kind when, on approaching the Highland line with its menacing mountains, he spoke to the young Englishman of what lay in that part of Scotland as a Scotsman as well as a Lowlander.

The modern traveller, as he makes the journey into the Highlands from the Lowland plains, will face a physical scene that has not changed, in its main outlines, much since the early days of the eighteenth century when the Bailie and other Southern Scots went North. As he leaves the Lowland towns behind him and comes to the wider and more deserted spaces of countryside under the shadow of the hills, the fact that he is travelling on a modern road will become somehow insignificant in these wide circumstances. The ramparts of the Highland line will hang over his advance in his motor car just as impressively as they did over the path of his forebears or of past travellers from England, on horseback or on foot. If he has any sentiment for scenery, any historical imagination, he will, just as much as those who went before him, feel that he is entering a strange new land. And if he presses more deeply into the true Highland country than the Bailie and his companion ever did, until he reaches the North and the West by the Atlantic Ocean, he will come to a country that is still wilder than ever they knew, still more apparently remote from the douce Lowlands than anything they ever experienced. Here, on the ultimate shores of the traditional land of the Gael, nature has not changed in thousands of years; nor has the sad recession of humanity from these valleys and from the beaches of these long sea lochs done anything save stress their essential immutability.

Immutable they may be in appearance, but how changed is the life that is left amongst them! In some parts of the Highlands of Scotland the deer and the fox and the badger and the mountain hare and the grouse and the hawk and the eagle still roam and fly and multiply in these free spaces, in this free air. But the men and the women that once shared this freedom with them are gone; and it is not only the fact of death that has removed them. Their bodies, evicted from their homelands and driven out from Scotland in their lifetime, lie in graves far from the Highlands; and their descendants who live are scattered all over the world. There are some parts of these Highlands of ours not three hours' driving from Glasgow where the desolation of the human scene is all but absolute. Only an isolated gamekeeper's cottage informs you that people can live here. Only the ruins of crofters' homes sinking back into the heather and the bracken, into the remorseless encroaching and absorbing hillsides, stay to remind you that they once not only lived here, but flourished after a fashion. That fashion was the old Gaelic way of life that provided the honest Glasgow Bailie of Scott's novel with the subject for hair-raising stories. One cannot but feel, however, that even he in his most practical and law-abiding mood would have been touched to sadness by such a scene. That remote strain of the Gregarach in him would have cried out in protest, and, what is equally important, the kindly Lowland Scot in him would have been moved to pity and indignation.

There are indeed some parts of the Gaelic lands that

28

have turned into these plague spots of natural beauty and human decay; and the tendency which has effected their transition is felt throughout all the Highlands. But in the inescapable mood of sadness which anyone of Celtic blood must feel when he looks upon this part of Scotland, it will not do to neglect the fact that life *does* continue and sometimes continues to struggle against increasing odds in other parts of these mountain and island regions. Still less will it do to imagine that, because the Gael has been so largely driven from his ancient geographical kingdom, the Celt is being driven out of the world as were the ghostly Picts before him. Far from it. But before considering these more cheerful things, it is necessary here to consider how it was that this huge eviction was imposed upon this proud, conservative, and most land-tenacious of races. How was it, to give but one striking instance, that there can exist in the Highlands one celebrated Strath that sent about one hundred soldiers (and what soldiers too!) to fight for the British against Napoleon, about fifty to fight for them at the Crimea, two in the war of 1914, and none in the last one?

The spectacular eradication of the Highlanders from their native land came about from two causes – political and economic circumstances and the pressure of those circumstances on the peculiar qualities of the Highlanders' nature.

The Highlander is proud, bold, emotional, yet formal. He is courteous by nature and tradition, is sensitive and is disgusted by insensitivity in others. It is as much for this reason of temperament as because of the clan system which linked the lowest with the highest, that the old-fashioned Highlander, however poor and shabby, always considered himself a gentleman – much to the merriment

29

of his Lowland compatriots. He is quick to take offence and is sometimes spontaneously and emotionally quick to forgive; more often he will nurse an injury to the grave. He is naturally and intensely poetic, expressing this quality in his own poetic and expressive Gaelic or in that form of English which he uses, much influenced by his native tongue. It would be a mistake to suppose that this poetry is all melancholy or martial. Sometimes it takes the form of humour, and very gay humour too, without bitterness. Your Highlander can be a very funny fellow. He has a childlike love of bright colours and pretty things, his visible art is ingenious, touching, and often gay. Childlike he is indeed in many ways, but it would again be a profound mistake to take the one-time popular Lowland and English view of him and confuse his childlike qualities with savagery. Anyone who studies his tradition should soon lose that illusion, particularly if he acquaints himself with the Gaelic language which is rich in the fruits of civilization as well as of age. He is conservative and devoted to his own land and people. Though the history of the Highlands is soaked in the blood of interclan warfare, and though the Highlanders made frequent raids upon their Lowland neighbours, it was their own homeland that was always uppermost in their minds; for they are not an imperially-minded or expansionist people. They are justly famed as soldiers; for their bravery is proverbial. In attack they are superb, but decline upon defence.

These on the whole attractive qualities have their weak sides. The Highlander's poetic contempt for material things has given him a reputation for dirt and disorder of a kind which passes the merely picturesque; it is a reputation which is not without foundation. His celebrated

sense of timelessness which may rest upon his view of
Eternity ('When God made time He made plenty of
it'), can have its charm. It can, however, degenerate into
a selfish disregard of other people's conveniences, interests, and even necessities. He can be really lazy, that is to
say negatively indolent in a mentally costive kind of way
without the positive pleasure of true relaxation. He can
be a formidable drunkard, but not, it must in justice be
said, usually in a violent and offensively extrovert
manner: alcohol is but one of his dreams. And (the best
being corrupted ...) his poetic tongue, or, to put it lower,
his verbal facility in English can be most effectively per-
verted to the uses of low cunning. His ineradicably
religious or spiritual temperament (even when he does
not adhere to any form of faith) seldom allows him to
commit the ultimate sin of despair, for he believes that
the eternal values will somehow put things right in eternity. He can, however, provide about as good an imita-
tion of the outward and visible signs of despair as you
are likely to find anywhere else in the world.

In this there lies his greatest, his most self-destructive
weakness – for weakness it is, and not a vice. It has
already been said that in attack he is strong and in defence he is weak. It has already been pointed out that he
has a fund of immaterial consolation on which he can
draw when the material attack upon him grows too
strong. It may well be understood, then, that his greatest
temptation when faced by crude, cruel material, men and
circumstances, over which even his bravery cannot, or
does not seem likely to prevail, is to withdraw too easily
into an inner world of his own thoughts, inactive, dignified, and doomed. Sometimes the old longing for action
will spring up in him again. He will thrust aside the

immaterial but heavy load of dreams and rush into the fray once more. Sometimes he will suffer defeat gloriously – as recently did the crofters who staked out their claims for land at Knoydart and who were overcome by circumstances beyond their control. Sometimes, alas! he will, with less glory but with equal dignity, sink back again into that inner world which he alone inhabits and in which it is to be presumed he finds some sad solace.

To the Scottish Gael who has emerged to learn something of the ways of this world, but who keeps his love for his people, even to the admirer of the Highlander who wishes him well without being of his kith and kin, this cardinal failing of the Scottish Highlander is infuriating. It can be worse than infuriating, it can be so depressing to observe that it may lead the onlooker actually to despair of there being any future for this people, a kind of despair, mark you, to which even the Gael himself has never completely succumbed. If the Highlands themselves are scattered with the plague spots of beautiful desolation, the history of the lovers of the Highlanders contains innumerable instances of those who have, perhaps unworthily, but perhaps equally understandably, 'given them up'.

This weakness of a retreat into himself is the reverse side of a good element in him which separates him from his cousin the Irish Gael – it is the greatest difference between them. The Irish Gael is one of the most delightful and agreeable of fellows under the sun; but he has one unworthy and indeed disagreeable quality, his unforgiving malice, his active and persistent grubbing hatred when he has been defeated or even only thwarted. This quality, none the less, has stiffened and helped him in his struggle for freedom, however much it may have loaded

his otherwise cheerful soul with acid. The Scottish Highlander has none of this. He is too dignified. If he is defeated
(and alas! he is all too easily convinced on that point) he
does not poison himself with endless dreams of revenge.
Nor (again alas!) does he do anything about it, but sinks
into himself. Thus by paradox the Irish Gael has been
helped towards his liberty by the better side of one of his
failings, while the Scottish Highlander has been reduced
and forced to succumb by the weaker side of one of his
virtues.

This, then, is the character of the Scottish Highlander.
It is a character which, for all its martial virtues and its
spiritual integrity, would have been a very difficult one in
any circumstances to defend and preserve in the last two
centuries. Anywhere in Europe a race such as the Scottish
Highlanders would have seemed to late Georgian eyes an
anachronism; to the Victorians, especially when they
found it in their own island of Great Britain, it seemed not
only an anachronism but an inconvenience. They, the
Georgians and the Victorians, proceeded to get rid of this
anachronism and inconvenience in this way:—

By the middle of the eighteenth century the old Highland way of life had been going on in that almost
clearly defined area known as the Highlands for hundreds
of years. Its half-independent existence had been an
annoyance to the Government of Scotland when the
country was itself independent: it was an annoyance that
was bequeathed to the Government of the United Kingdom at Westminster in 1707. It was an annoyance that
would probably have been got rid of by the advance (if
one grants that such an advance was inevitable) of British
industrialism, British capitalism, British centralization,
and, in the end, the long end, British Socialism. The old

Highland way of life might have defended itself against many things, but not against such as these. But the process of getting rid of it might have taken some time. As it was, that process was shortened by something (in modern eyes) so unimportant as a dynastic struggle. The Georgians took the occasion of the failure of Jacobitism in Scotland to try to rid the Highlands of Scotland of Highlanders. And, though Jacobitism was utterly dead by the time Queen Victoria came to the throne, all subsequent, more superficially peaceful and certainly more hypocritical attempts towards the same end by the Victorians derived from this first blow.

In 1745 Prince Charles Edward Stuart, grandson of James VII of Scotland and II of England, who had been driven from his kingdoms in 1688, landed in the West Highlands of Scotland to make the last attempt to regain the Crown of the United Kingdom for his family. He was joined by a number of Highland chiefs and raised a small but formidable Highland army. He marched south and east, defeated the English Hanoverian General Cope and took possession of Edinburgh. Here he lingered for two months, the last Stuart to hold Court in the Palace of Holyroodhouse. He then marched into England and came to Derby. When the news of this reached London it threw the English Capital into a panic; but Charles, yielding to the advice of his Highland officers who now found themselves far from home, turned back into Scotland. He fought delaying and rearguard actions until he reached the 'Capital of the Highlands', Inverness. Here the full weight of the Hanoverian army, under the Duke of Cumberland, came up with him. At Culloden, a few miles outside of Inverness, Cumberland decisively defeated Charles, all but obliterating his Highland army, forcing the Prince into a flight amongst the heather, and eventually into an exile which endured for the rest of his life.

This, in brief, is the celebrated story of 'the '45', which has been told at length and in full detail in innumerable books of history and in separate studies. It has inspired a wealth of romance in story, poetry, and song, and has haunted the imagination of romantic Scots for two hundred years. That this romantic feeling has been justly inspired cannot be denied. Even the most violent Whig denigrators would admit that the whole episode had the elements of heroism and romance. However, even the most fervent admirer of the Prince to-day would also have to admit that much of the romantic writing (some of it pretending to be factual) and much of the romantic sentiments left behind in the two centuries after 'the '45' is false, sentimental, and meretricious. This transmutation of an heroic episode into 'a tale for greensick girls' has naturally inspired reaction quite separate from the political opposition to Jacobitism. There are writers in Scotland who still spend quite an appreciable portion of their working time in discovering facts and theories that can cry down the Rising and rob it of its attraction as a story. Some, indeed, are so eager in this pursuit that they will deny that 'the '45' had any importance at all, claiming that it was an unimportant and bloody episode soon disposed of. This is pushing that strange enthusiasm for denigration too far; for, whatever may be the inner history of the Rising, its failure indubitably killed the old Highland way of life in the Highlands and utterly altered the social structure of half Scotland.

After his victory at Culloden, the Duke of Cumberland, with characteristic Teutonic savagery, took the most ferocious reprisals, not only against the wounded remnants of the Prince's army, but against the people of the Highlands. Tales of his butchery still survive and at the time spread quickly all over Scotland, arousing sympathy even amongst those antipathetic to the Jacobite cause. This sympathy, genuine in itself, may well have provided the beginning of an emotion, an attitude of mind which was to degenerate into sentimentality in after years, the romantic tenderness of the Lowlander for the Highlander – when he is not dangerous. When Cumberland went back to London he had done his best to 'smoke out the nest of savages', but even his most strenuous efforts could not positively kill off the majority of the Highlanders. It was left to the Government in 1747, after his return, to complete his work with the deadliest blow yet struck at the Highlands.

George II's Government rightly understood that the most effective way of destroying the Highlands was not by force of arms, but by depriving the Highlanders of the age-old structure of their way of life. To this end they forbade the carrying of arms and the wearing of the distinctive Highland dress, and enforced this prohibition vigorously and effectively. These may seem trivial matters to us to-day, but they struck deep at the Highlander's most vulnerable point, his pride, and did much to deprive him of hope. Even more potent was the Government's destruction of the clan system. They deprived even such chiefs as were not exiled of their hereditary powers of jurisdiction and abolished all tenures of land by war-holding. The legal, military, and social structure of the Highlands was thus destroyed by an act of Parliament in London; and from 1747 (except that he was of sheer necessity allowed to speak Gaelic) the Highlander became as all other Scots. Queen Margaret's work was finished.

But the saintly Queen would not have approved of what followed. Deprived of their way of life, deprived of hope, the Highlander's incapacity in dogged defence at once discovered itself. They began to leave their native land in large numbers. This exodus may have been partly voluntary, but it was in a large measure brought about by the pressure amounting sometimes to forcible eviction exerted by the Government, who were only too glad to see as many Highlanders as possible cast up upon Transatlantic shores.

It is with shame that one sets it down, but it must be recorded that in this they found help from the Highland chiefs themselves – even from some of those who had fought for the Prince, been exiled and in later years returned to their estates. Highland gentlemen who in the latter half of the eighteenth century found themselves owning several hundred square miles of mountain and moorland territory did not see much use in keeping upon this land human inhabitants who were no longer allowed to fight for them and who could pay only very small rents for their smallholdings. Sheep, and later deer and sporting rights, would prove much more profitable. No doubt there were some of these landlords who did convince themselves that in sending their tenants to Canada and America they were lifting them out of an impossible position and were opening a brave new world to them. If so, their convictions must have been very strong to have withstood the lamentations that filled their wide lands a each emigrant ship departed for the 'Golden West', filled with the descendants of those who for a thousand years had followed their own forefathers in war and peace. Some of these lamentations were turned into the loveliest and most poignant of Gaelic poetry and song. Even to-day

37

it is impossible to listen to them unmoved. For anyone of Highland blood it is sometimes unbearable. The Highland chiefs whose actions provoked them must indeed have had strong convictions.

In the nineteenth century Jacobitism was dead; and the political pressure to evict the Highlanders ceased. Except for looking upon them as an occasional reserve for the drawing of excellent soldiers, the Government, in the modern phrase, 'could not have cared less' about what went on in the Highlands. They left the management of such affairs to the landowning classes. These classes now began to be implemented by rich incomers who bought up estates for sporting or investment purposes. These incomers had not even the faint scruples of the hereditary landlords to overcome. They were therefore just as ruthless in their policy of economic eviction. One looks upon their depredations upon our country with distress, but not with that disgust with which one views the hypocrisy of the now thoroughly *déraciné* chiefs.

This disgust is at its strongest when one recalls the behaviour of the Duchess of Sutherland. This lady's estates, which covered a large part of the shire from which she took her title, offered in the first half of the nineteenth century the worst examples of enforced emigration and of ruthless eviction in all the Highlands. To-day, a century of more afterwards, the utter desolation of Sutherland with its strange, sad beauty, its decaying stumps of erstwhile human habitation, speaks more eloquently than could any words of the deeds of the eviction period. The depredations of Her Grace's factors were so ruthless and widespread that, even in that period, they aroused comment slightly more forceful than Gaelic poetic lamentation, and there were criticisms uttered in Lowland and

English newspapers. The Duchess was not restrained by these, but was moved to defend herself. She hired the services of Harriet Beecher Stowe, the celebrated American authoress of *Uncle Tom's Cabin*, to write for her a book proving that in expelling crofters from the glens which their ancestors had inhabited for centuries and in burning down their houses over their heads when they showed reluctance to go, she was animated by the most humanitarian motives. She merely wished to get these poor people out of a backward way of life and to open to them the door of progress in the New World. This commission was accepted; and in a volume called *Happy Memories* the author of 'the book that had freed the black slaves in America' pleaded the cause of those who treated the Celtic Highlanders in Scotland like slaves. It is small wonder that that widely distributed nursery book, *Uncle Tom's Cabin*, is less popular in the Highlands than in any other part of Great Britain.

Throughout the remainder of the century the tide of emigration continued. If the number of enforced evictions declined, it was due less to awakening consciences than to the fact that so many 'clearances' had now been made that many landowners were satiated with their depredations and did not need more land. In the 1880's, however, the question unexpectedly flared up again. The island of Skye, already becoming known to tourists as a 'beauty spot', was subjected to a sudden series of enforced evictions of the same kind as those that had earlier taken place in Sutherland – though not of quite so violent an order.

The Highland character is incalculable. Some almost forgotten fighting spirit was suddenly aroused in the crofters who had without more than verbal protest endured this treatment for a century. There were riots, and the Government of the day sent a battleship into Portree harbour to restore order. The present writer well remembers from his elder relatives' accounts of how old women from the glens came down to the seashore and, filling their stockings with stones to beat them off, awaited the advent of the sailors, who, to do them justice, had not the faintest idea of what it was all about.

This incident succeeded in arousing or at least catching the attention of public opinion. People in the South at last became aware of what had been going on in the Highlands, and there was a certain amount of genuine and generous indignation. There may have been the usual element of political manoeuvring in the Englishman Joseph Chamberlain's much publicized Highland speeches in Glasgow and Inverness, in which he made popular the political battle-cry of 'three acres and a cow', but there was also the usual mixture of true emotion in his actions which that strange man always possessed. His audiences were certainly animated by true and vocal feeling.

This feeling was sufficiently vocal to be heard in a place so remote from the Highland scene as Westminster; and in 1886 the Crofters' Holding Act ('relating to the tenure of land by crofters in the Highlands and Islands of Scotland') was passed. This Act established 'The Crofters' Commission', which was empowered to guard the crofters' rights not only in his historic holding of his land but in the fixing of fair rents by his landlord. In 1911 'the Statutory Small Tenants' Act' abolished the Crofters' Commission and put in its place the permanent Land Court. This Act also, and in other ways, defined and protected more securely the rights of smallholders in general in the Gaelic parts of Scotland. It is, incidentally, significant that it was laid down that at least one member of the original Commission had to be a Gaelic speaker. This might be described as the first Parliamentary recognition since 1746 of the language as a respectable factor in the life of Scotland. By 1911 this was a fact that was taken for granted. The effect of these two Acts (further extended and defined in 1919) can, without going into the minutiae of legal terms, be summed up thus: the crofter or Highland smallholder's right to the land for which he pays rent to his landlord is now fixed in himself and in his family. This applies whether his landlord is the historic 'chief of his clan', a more recent incomer, or the Government itself. In a sentence, his rights in his land are now entailed upon him and his heirs. He can no longer be dispossessed in the old shameful way.

And so, at last, those that remain of the indigenous Highland peasantry have acquired a tenure of their historic land which is more secure than that possessed by any other of the peasantry in Great Britain. It was a truly Liberal and, on the whole, altruistic action on the part of two Liberal Governments to pass these measures. And something of the obstinate predilection of the Scots for the unfashionable political creed of Liberalism may spring from a recognition of it, particularly in the Highlands.

Maybe; but there were not wanting those, particularly amongst the opponents of the Liberals, who were quick to claim that it was all too late, that the Highlandman's spirit in the Highlands was now broken and that to give him a plot of land in his ancestral glen was merely to give him somewhere to decay in mournful peace. And it was with these lugubrious prognostications in the Highland air, uttered by so many authorities who 'really knew' the

Highlander and his ways, that the first World War broke out. Nevertheless, the United Kingdom was once more able to call upon what remained of the youth of this allegedly degenerate race to provide a small nucleus of what still remained amongst the finest soldiery in Europe.

'It is too late. The Highland crofter is finished. There is no place for him in the modern world; and even if there were, he wouldn't take it, for he is now sunk into hopeless laziness. Look at the people who have tried to help him. Look at ...' This kind of remark is often heard to-day, not only from the capitalist, irritated by the Highlander's refusal to help him in his money-making plans, but also from supporters of the 'Welfare State' in whose schemes the independent smallholder has no place. However repugnant such statements on such lips may be to one, there are certain moments of depression when one admits to oneself that these people may be right, but for the wrong reasons. One returns to a West Highland community which in one's own lifetime sent fifty children to school, and now only numbers half a dozen. One sees the croft falling into desuetude, no longer because of forced eviction or social pressure but through an internal inanition in the community itself. One sees, and on all sides hears of, the continual exodus of youth to the towns and overseas.

One may turn for spiritual refreshment, for the melancholy pleasure of summoning up 'remembrance of things past', to the old people with their old ways and their Gaelic speech. Here, indeed, one will meet again the old courtesy, the old poetic imagery in talk, the old acuteness of mind, and sometimes even flashes of the old humour, if not gaiety, of the natural Highlander. But it can hardly be said that such an experience is an invigorating one for

nyone who looks towards the future of the Highlands
vith hope. There is too often in these old people a Nir-
ana-like acceptance of the decline of their way of life, a
apacity for agreeing with whatever you say, a way of
.ccepting without struggle any contrary circumstances,
iowever trivial and easy to deal with; in short, what the
ialf-charmed, half-irritated Saxon would call bone-
aziness. However much one may say to oneself, and with
eal conviction, that it is not bone-laziness as the South-
rner means it, but the age-old habit of the Celt of retreat-
ng into himself when faced with intolerable circum-
tances, the effect on the future of the Highlander in the
Iighlands will be, one gloomily admits, the same –
)eath.

It is not that one blames him. Indeed, one is perhaps
nly too ready to think of excuses for him. For two hun-
lred years he has been consistently and remorselessly
ittacked by means of weapons he cannot resist economi-
ally, politically, and socially. He has been wounded in
is most vulnerable parts, his pride, his loyalty, and his
ove for his land. Is not the miracle that, by means of this
atal retreat into himself, he has been able to keep so
;ood-humoured? Is it not a miracle that there are any of
iis kind left here at all? The attack on him has been
erocious, and his temperament has been peculiarly sus-
.eptible to that form of attack. His circumstances and his
emperament have doomed him. Thus one ends one's
lepressing reflexions with a depressing excuse as one
eaves him upon some fine autumn day (that season of
insurpassed beauty in the Highlands) pottering about his
:roft, smoking in his doorway, or gazing at some fishing-
iets that need mending, a solitary figure in the autumn of
iis days and, so it seems, in the late autumn of his race.

43

To give in to such moods is to surrender to the modern capitalist a modern socialist view of the Highlander far more completely than he himself has ever surrendered to their attacks. And before we begin to celebrate the Highland Gael's obsequies, thus paying the ultimate tribute to his diverse enemies, it is as well to consider certain facts about the general position of the Scottish Gael to-day general as opposed to the admittedly many and sad but particular instances of his decline in the Highlands. And in that general conspectus let not such signs of hope as do exist beyond the Highland line be forgotten. Let us consider, first, the Gael in the whole country of Scotland.

As soon as the traveller crosses the Border from England into Scotland he will observe Highland names over the shops of even the smallest Lowland towns. And when he reaches the larger cities, still in the Lowlands, this becomes even more obvious. According to the Registry, one in every eight of the inhabitants of Edinburgh bear distinctively Highland names. Racial statistics built upon names are notoriously unreliable; but when one considers that the number of people with Highland nomenclature in Edinburgh two hundred years ago was very much smaller – less than half in proportion – one is entitled to a fairly safe inference: these people who have increased the proportion of Highland names in Edinburgh in the last two hundred years must have descended from immigrants from the Highlands. And even this rough-and-ready method of assessing the Highlanders in Edinburgh does not take into account these bearing an equal amount of Highland blood through the female line with Lowland names.

Edinburgh has been chosen as an example of infiltration from the Highlands, not because it is the Capital of

Scotland, but because it has always been an essentially Lowland town. It is far more Lowland than London is 'South of England'. It would be unfair to cite Glasgow, indubitably the Celtic Capital of Great Britain: its population is too mixed and floating. But in nearly every other Lowland city and town in the north-east, as well as in the south and west, something of the same proportion of Highland names and families of Highland origin can be found as in Edinburgh.

This is but one sign of a fact that may not be generally recognized by those who bewail the 'death of the Highlands', the fact that by no means all of those who have left or been evicted from the land of the Gael have been lost to Scotland. By no means all the Highland Celts who have left their ancestral hills have gone to Canada, America, or London.

It is true that those who have gone far South or even further overseas have not unnaturally tended to stress their origin and keep it alive. It is true that thereby the Highlander in London, Toronto, and New York gives the impression that (apart from Glasgow, which is a special case) he is the only true Highlander who has left the Highlands. In point of fact, since the wall of the Highland line went down there are just as many Highlanders who have come South and East and yet remained in their own country, if not in their own land. In an entirely unspectacular and, for the most part, unselfconscious way, they have permeated the Lowlands of Scotland far more effectively than they have the distant lands where they always form a conscious unit amongst other units. There are, of course, conscious Celtic units in every Lowland town in the form of Highland Societies admirable in intent and enthusiastically supported; but a far more

potent if quieter Highland influence on the South o
Scotland has been the steady influence of Highland blood

Another interesting and cheering influence has beer
the changed attitude all over Scotland to the Gaelic
language and Highland customs. This is a change that
has taken place forcibly and completely and within
living memory. It has been said earlier on that in Victorian times many a Highland student at Edinburgh
University would conceal his knowledge of Gaelic. Part
of this may have been due to natural reserve; part was
also due to his suspicion that his Lowland fellow-students
might despise him for speaking what they looked upon as
a remote and savage tongue. Nowadays this would be
impossible. The possessor of Gaelic is now positively
envied in all intelligent circles in Scotland. Sometimes
maybe this envy (or more charitably admiration) may
spring from falsely romantic ideas, but more often it is
the product of a late awakening respect for the ancient
tongue itself. Here, people feel, is something still surviving in our country which is indubitably and absolutely
Scottish. Some of its Lowland admirers too can perceive,
even though they may not apprehend, its qualities of
forceful and poetic expression. Most educated Lowlanders nowadays know a few Gaelic words and phrases,
nearly all can exchange a greeting or give a toast in something that passes for Gaelic. Classes for the learning of
Gaelic have sprung up in the most unexpected Lowland
quarters; and the Gaelic lessons given on the Scotitsh
B.B.C. have proved one of the most successful ventures
that peculiar hybrid has ever put upon the Scottish air.

Highland customs in the Lowlands are naturally less
easy to define, but there is one of them that cannot be
allowed to pass without comment – the wearing of the

kilt. This famous garment has had many strange vicissitudes. Without going into tedious details, it may be safely stated that the philabeg, or short kilt, derived from the larger and less-determinate garment the *féiladh-mór*, which had been worn by all classes of men in the Highlands for centuries and was as distinctive to them in Scotland as was their Gaelic speech. After the suppression of the Rising of 1745 it was forbidden. Upon the raising of the Highland regiments under the Hanoverians, however, the philabeg was wisely allowed and encouraged by the military authorities – but only for soldiers fighting for King George III. And as such it might have survived solely as a curiosity of regional military uniform.

It enjoyed, however, an unexpected civilian revival and was patronized in the most unusual quarters. By the beginning of the nineteenth century, the Highlands were pacified and such Highlanders as remained in them were innocuous enough to be ripe in that romantic period for romantic exploitation. The genius of Sir Walter Scott spread the fame of the kilted Highlander all over Europe; and the seal might be said to have been set upon this conception of Celtic Scotland when, upon his first visit to Scotland in 1824, George IV wrapped his podgy legs in a kilt. The effect was immediate. Every gentleman with estates in the Highlands, whether he was of Scottish or Levantine origin, instantly felt obliged to don the kilt and sometimes to invent a suitable tartan. His lead was often followed by romantically-minded people who, though they lived in the Lowlands, could trace a faint Highland ancestry. This partly romantic, partly comical revival was, however, a purely upper- or wealthy-class affair. No Highland crofter would ever have dreamed of donning the garment of his ancestors now worn by such strange immigrants. And the only working-class Highlanders occasionally seen in it were those servants (Queen Victoria's John Brown is an example) who were dressed up by their employers.

So it remained for nearly a century – an attractive, gay, colourful, but purely class and often snobbish badge of dress. It had curious side developments, of course. Comedians popularized it upon the music-hall stage. The designers of coloured picture postcards spread all over the world the concept of the kilted Scot and his 'banging saxpence', and small boys from the middle classes in all parts of Scotland wore it, with an incongruous Eton collar as a 'Sunday best'. The final touch of well-meaning absurdity was provided when a society of little Cockney girls in a suburb of London were taught to play the pipes and toured the country dressed up in the essentially masculine garb of the Scottish Highlander.

Then after the war of 1914–18 this historic dress enjoyed a second and much healthier revival. The longing for the countryside, the open air which released so many town-dwellers almost simultaneously all over Europe, affected Scotland profoundly. Very sensibly the lads from Glasgow, Edinburgh, Dundee, Aberdeen, and other Lowland towns, who went walking holidays in their own adjacent Highlands, decided to adopt the comfortable and traditional Highland dress for their expeditions. In a year or two the kilt had become, without any class feeling and without too many elaborate questions about 'the right to wear it', the popular holiday garment for a large part of the young men of Scotland. These lads were often followed by their middle-aged seniors of Nationalist tendencies, who seized upon the occasion of holidays to imitate their bolder and perhaps less self-conscious juniors. Thus, though the indigenous Highland crofter sticks conservatively to his 'breeks', the descendants of many other Highland crofters who emigrated to the Lowlands long ago have now returned, even more conservatively and with some gusto, to the 'Garb of Old Gaul'. In this way, quite naturally and without affectation, the kilt has become for a large part of Scotland a democratically national male dress.

This, then, has been the influence of the dispersed Highlanders on the country of Scotland as a whole – the influence of Highland blood in the Lowlands, the increased respect for the Gaelic tongue throughout Scotland, and the spreading of certain Highland customs of which the wearing of the kilt is the most obvious. This influence has been almost entirely beneficial to Scotland. If there be any rigid Scots, Highland or Lowland, who object to it on the grounds that there is an essential and unbridgeable dichotomy in Scotland, that 'the Highlander is as different from the Lowlander as the Lowlander is from the Englishman', let them reflect that when the Gaels retreated into their hills they did *not* form a separate nation, that when the Highlanders were in exile after the Jacobite Risings they were passionately and implacably Scottish as well as Highland. Let them recall also that most unforgettable of all Lowland characters in Scottish story, the character already referred to in this chapter, Scott's Bailie Nicol Jarvie, and in recalling him let them remember the hidden feeling for his Highland cousins that ran irrepressibly in that honest Glasgow merchant's blood. It is a feeling which now need no longer be hidden.

And what of the Highlander in the Highlands? Even here where desolation and near-despair, combined with native inanition, seemed twenty or thirty years ago to have done their work, it will not do to follow the Capitalist or Socialist lead, shrug your shoulders and say that 'the game is up'. Even here there are signs that the new-found national feeling that is everywhere appearing in Scotland may yet express itself in action, in deeds as well as in words, and in romantic musings. The Highlands are very much on Scotland's conscience to-day.

It is possible that the Crofters' and Smallholders' Acts of 1886 and 1911 came too late; but they were at least practical as well as well-meant attempts to set right an ancient wrong. It is possible that the now widespread respect for the Gaelic language and Gaelic customs may be seen to its best advantage in Scotland as a whole, but it cannot have been without its effect on the indigenous Gaels who now have the right to Gaelic education in their schools and a Gaelic service on the wireless. It is true that the Hydro-Electric Board for Scotland, which intends to use our Highland water power for its purposes, is primarily concerned with industrial matters, but at least its supporters have put it forward as one of their first objects of management that they should give employment to the Highlanders in the Highlands. It is possible that this may be mostly window-dressing, but even so it is significant of a popular feeling that they thought it worth while to dress this window in this particular way. It is possible that other schemes for the employment of the Highland people without driving them out of their native land may be partly inspired by mixed motives, but at least another part of them openly proclaims a laudable object as its first object.

It is possible, in short, to say that the conscience of Scotland about the Highlanders in the Highlands may have awakened to action too late and in too vague a way. It is equally possible to believe that it may yet help to save what remains of our living Gaelic culture, not as a romantic and empty shell, nor as a museum piece, but as a way of life for living men and women. ... It is possible.

CHAPTER THREE

THE GREAT DIVISION

2. *The Lowlands and the Lowlanders*

THE Lowlands of Scotland and those who live in them have provided almost as much matter for sentimental and comical misrepresentation as have the Highlands and the Highlanders. The Highland scene (though it is scarcely possible to overpraise it at its rarest and most exquisite) is often held up for popular admiration at its most blatant and at its worst. It is significant of this sentimental attitude that it should have put forward as a kind of flag of attack for the particular beauty of the Highlands a representation of a hillside entirely covered in puce – the heather in bloom, and that it should hold up for romantic admiration what can perhaps best be described as the puce elements in the Highlander himself.

In the same way, but in order to provide a contrast, the Lowlands of Scotland are often popularly represented as being profoundly dour, grey, and sensationally depressing. And, to continue the antithesis in the human scene, the Lowlander is put forward as grim, humourless, and unemotional – in short, the complete unromantic opposite of his romantic Highland neighbour and compatriot. However, by one of those odd quirks of the mind which allow people to take, almost at the same time, contradictory views of the same thing, there is prevalent a good deal of pawky sentimentality about the Lowland character.

This sentimentality springs from and was encouraged by the 'Kailyard' literature at the end of the last century. This literature is much blown upon now, and is held up by the more ardent of our new writers for especial contempt. It was, it must be admitted, highly sentimental, often false, and to a Scot often very irritating. We are, however, now far enough from it to be able to look back upon it objectively and to recognize a certain emotional charm in it. Moreover, there was about it artistry of a kind. It will not do to dismiss the novels of Ian Maclaren (whose real name was Watson*), the pleasant stories of Annie S. Swan, and the sentimental songs of Harry Lauder (who was in a part of the character he showed to the world the minstrel of the Kailyarders) as nothing but lucrative gush. There was too much talent in them for that, too much real feeling.

And with the mention of this word 'feeling' one is reminded of an inescapable fact about the Lowland character which these now dead talented sentimentalizers were sentimentalizing. Whatever one may think of the view the Kailyarders were giving to the outside world of their compatriots, we must admit that they were not inventing on the basis of nothing. Underneath his restrained and sometimes grim exterior the Lowland Scot is a deeply emotional character; and any emotion can turn into sentimentality or be the subject of sentimentality – but this is to anticipate.

It is necessary to repeat here and most emphatically that it is a great mistake to think of the Highlands as the

* This fact is not mentioned in any spirit of denigration of the Reverend, wholly Scottish and Highland Mr Watson, but merely to preserve the author from any accusation of having called upon the name out of 'clannishness'.

North of Scotland and the Lowlands as the South, for some of the most characteristically Lowland parts of Scotland in scenery and in population lie well to the North. Indeed, there is a case to be made out for saying that you do not reach the pure Lowlands until you have penetrated to the north-east of Aberdeenshire, wherein you will find the sharpest Lowland antithesis to the Highlands, even though those parts are two hundred miles north-east of Ben Lomand, and even further north of some purely Highland Celtic Hebridean isles. The Lowlands lie east and south of a line drawn roughly diagonally up Scotland from the Mull of Galloway to the tip of Buchan: they thus occupy nearly half of the physical space of the mainland. To the far north-east in Caithness and in Orkney and Shetland the land and the people are most certainly not Highland or Celtic, and they do share some characteristics with the Lowlands. But the origins of the inhabitants are Norse, and there is still a strongly Norse influence in their way of life. It would be quite wrong then to include these lands in the generic term, the Lowlands, just because they are Scottish without being Highland.

The true Lowlands of Scotland cover the best part of some twenty counties, including the minute Clackmannan, as well as the ample Aberdeenshire, containing as well the four major cities of Scotland – Edinburgh, Glasgow, Aberdeen, and Dundee. Anyone who has had any experience, then, of the diversity of the small country of Scotland need scarcely be told that a countryside covering the majority of twenty Scottish shires, and holding almost the entire industrial population, will be far from uniform. Indeed, anyone who knows and loves the Lowlands would claim, and with some justification, that there

is much more diversity in them than in the more roman-
ticized other half of Scotland, the Highlands and Islands.
Nonetheless there undoubtedly is a general Lowland
character in the Lowland scene, human, natural, and
architectural, which is as strong as the taste of a root
flavouring in a salad made from many ingredients. That
general characteristic is austerity. It is an austerity with
so many subtle undertones, so many subtle and sometimes
paradoxical variations in it, that when you come to know
the Lowlands well you may begin to forget the austerity in
your enjoyment of the diversities and paradoxes, and may
even persuade yourself that there is a richness of subtle
character in the Lowland scene and the Lowland character which is lacking in the more obvious appeal of the
nation to the South.

Still, there is no doubt that it is a sense of austerity that
falls like a douche of cold water (refreshing or depressing
according to his mood) on the traveller from England
who approaches Scotland from the Lowlands Border
country and for the first time. It is an austerity which will
follow him if he travels northwards from the Border,
keeping to the Lowland side of the country. For all her
magnificence he will find that the first note that Edinburgh strikes in her always majestic chord of music is one
of austerity. The ancient land of Fife, with its ancient
capital of St Andrews, is beautiful and austere. Across the
waters of the Tay, Dundee, once an ancient city, now a
grim but vital legacy of nineteenth century industrialism,
is something rather more than austere. Further on, Angus
and Kincardine, though slightly under a waft from the
Highland hills, are austere in a remote kind of way. England with her soft luxuriance seems very far away here.
And by the time he has passed through the quiet greens

and greys and dull reds of the Aberdeenshire agricultural country, and reached the superb silver self-sufficiency of the city of Aberdeen itself, it will be difficult for him to believe that he is still in the same island as that which contains Gloucestershire, Devon, or even the Midlands of England.

Further north still, north and east of Aberdeen, there is the ultimate Lowland land of Buchan washed upon two sides by the grey North Sea, and open to every wind from Norway and the Russian Steppes. Here, indeed, is the very essence of Scottish austerity in the physical scene. It is not, strictly speaking, an unfruitful land; and those who farm it with such unremitting persistence wring from the soil a living that is far from altogether harsh or penurious. Still there is in these ultimate Lowlands an atmosphere which has seldom if ever been better described than in Sir Alexander Gray's notable verses. No doubt many an honest prosperous Buchan farmer would object to some of the barer and more 'ungrateful' epithets in it; no doubt the poet was thinking of more than one corner of his country when he called his poem 'Scotland', but is was from the North-East that he sprang; and it is the North-East that is in these lines:–

> Here in the uplands
> The soil is ungrateful;
> The fields red with sorrel,
> Are stony and bare.
> A few trees, wind-twisted –
> Or are they but bushes ? –
> Stand stubbornly guarding
> A home here and there.
>
> Scooped out like a saucer,
> The land lies before me;

The waters, once scattered,
Flow orderly now
Through fields where the ghosts
Of the marsh and the moorland
Still ride the old marches
Despising the plough.

And yet within this wide austerity that begins at the Borders and goes by the North Sea to Buchan Ness, this austerity of grey landscape and grey architecture, there is for those who know and love this land an infinity of diversity, which can sometimes become almost luxuriant.

It would be difficult to find in Great Britain, possibly in all Western Europe, a countryside more naturally sour in appearance than the land in the lowland that lies directly between Edinburgh and Glasgow. This is not solely due to the squalid little industrial or mining towns which indeterminately scatter the route, nor to the slag heaps that insult the skyline in nearly every direction in which one looks and fill the air with their curious smell of mineral putrefaction. It springs also from something in the quality of the yellow-green or grey-green grass and from the mean little dirty-coloured burns that trickle (or swollenly and muddily empty themselves) into the Firth of Forth or the larger rivers. One cannot but feel that, even before man did his worst in this belt between Scotland's two greatest cities, it was a part of the country in which austerity had been so long indigenous that it had grown rancid with the years and had declined into the sourest form of Nature's puritanism. Nor does the sight of an occasional rotting Peel Tower, a decaying lairdling's house, relieve one's depression at the sight of the mean and squalid architecture of nineteenth-century industrialism that lines one's journey.

57

Here are the Lowlands at their very nadir of grim austerity and joylessness. Yet a few miles to the south and to the north of this sad strip of land there is countryside which, though it may have the essential austerity of the Lowlands, is as beautiful as this is ugly.

There are moorlands which, though bare of much cultivation and almost treeless, are full of a soft variety of colours and are shaped in their hill contours with a feminine softness. There are moorland streams and burns with water as bright and clear as any that you will find in the West Highlands, yet with a domestic douceness about them lacking in the more volatile northern waters. They flow not only through hill valleys and open moor spaces but in the end through fields and farm lands, some even, in an almost English fashion, by the very farms and villages themselves. There are the Ochil Hills, visible from Edinburgh, and the Campsie Fells that can be seen from Glasgow – little Highlands within, and essentially of, the Lowlands. There is true Border country with its strange mixture of wildness and farm land, domesticity and a pervading air of historic mystery that is as haunting as that to be found in any of the Celtic lands. There is the agricultural land of Ayrshire in the South and West as rich, if never as lush, as land in England.

And in the very furthest south and west there is that half-forgotten and most indefinable quarter known as Galloway, containing the shires of Kirkcudbright and Wigtown. Is it quite fair to include this southern projection of Scotland into the Atlantic Ocean and the Irish Sea amongst the Lowlands? Is there really any affinity between the bare beauty of Liddesdale and Teviotdale and this all but cut off, three parts island of Galloway, with its coloured mountains and wild hill lochs so reminiscent of the Highlands, its warm soft climate, its palm trees and exotic plants, more characteristic of Torquay than of Scotland? The answer to both questions is yes. For even this most Southern and Western outpost of Scotland shares a Lowland quality with the far North West of Buchan. Even here, amidst the palm trees and the coloured hills and the flats and the estuaries there is a note of austerity which separates the place from England on the one hand and the Celtic Highlands on the other. What an enchanting eccentricity Galloway is in the Lowlands of Scotland, yet how essentially linked it is with the essential centre!

The way of building (for it would sometimes be a little grandiose to call it architecture) of these various Lowlands of Scotland also expresses, and in a varied way, the austerity, both beautiful and ugly, of these countrysides. Compared with the average English village even the most rural Scottish Lowland equivalent is, if not actually unlovely, forbidding.

Here are no winding village streets, no clusters of haphazard houses that have grown up with the centuries round a church which in its own style of building, and its pleasant if not always beautiful accretions, marks the slow process of time. Instead there is usually one straight main street of grey little dwelling-places that seem to have sprung up for purely utilitarian purposes on either side of a road going straight through the country. Sometimes these houses proclaim through their square rugged stone fronts a decent eighteenth-century origin (seldom an earlier one) and sometimes they belong to an indeterminately later period. But they all achieve the same effect. They are solid, undecorative, severe, and individual, seeming to have been brought together by design and not by the growth of a homogeneous community. The

Kirk, whose tinny bell summons the worshippers on Sabbath mornings and evenings with a peculiarly un-mellifluous clangour, may be an ancient foundation, but it was not only the zeal and rage of long-dead reformers that destroyed the outward and visible signs of that foundation. In most cases it has been the nineteenth-century builders who have obliterated the past by overlaying it with the worst elements of Victorian suburban ecclesiastical architecture.

And as for the pub or inn, which in an English village is not only so full of charm but is, along with the church, an essential element of the place, here the contrast is to be seen and felt at its most poignant. Bare and unfurnished as a station waiting-room, decorated only by the crudest advertisements for spirits and tobacco, it possesses only too often an air of furtiveness and unfriendliness imposed upon it by being the public place of sin in a small community. To the traveller who stops for refreshment it seems to say 'there's just time for a quick one' (that melancholy exhortation which hangs over our age in more than matters only of refreshment). 'This is the place to get it; then be on your way. It's lucky that no one knows you here.'

The small industrial towns and villages that have sprung up unconnected with each other in the Lowlands in the last century under the impetus of uncontrolled Victorian individualism are, of course, even more unsympathetic in appearance and atmosphere. Such places, such products of those times, are anywhere usually fairly depressing. Let it suffice to say that in Scotland the small industrial town of a hundred years old reaches a pitch of forbidding grimness which surpasses even the industrial districts of Lancashire and the West Riding of Yorkshire.

One is relieved only by the fact that in Scotland the grimness is intensely concentrated and is not, as in England, spread over a vast desert of mean building stretching from village to village, town to town. It is nearly always possible from the main street of a Lowland Scottish mining village to lift your eyes from the grey, almost majestic grimness of the main street to the equally grey and undoubted majestic freedom of the surrounding Scottish countryside.

And in that surrounding Scottish countryside, and in the furthest part of the Lowlands, there are the buildings of men which are truly worthy of it. At least they are natural to it and seem, as are the valley fields and the dykes on the hills, not to be imposed decorations but fruits (albeit man-cultured rather than man-made) of the land and the landscape itself. There are solid but rambling farmhouses that have grown up from the centre of their surrounding fields, adding with the centuries, sometimes with the generations, touch by touch, the passing fashions of rural Scottish ways of building, and expressing in their humble manner the history of the countryside itself. There are small cottages standing boldly out or hidden in the folds of the Border or Aberdeenshire hills, lonely, individual, small, four-square, and proud they are of the essence of Scotland and of the Scottish Lowlands. One sees them from the hillside as they light their windows in the evening and one recalls Stevenson's magical phrase from a poem (what does it matter that it was written about another part of Scotland?), 'Lo, the hollow valley, lamp be-starred', and one's heart is moved to an atavistic sympathy for the way these Scottish forefathers built for themselves in these lonely places.

There are the Peel Towers of the Borders, the old keeps,

the old castles sometimes preserved, sometimes fallen into a decay which is not inharmonious with the landscape itself. There are also those houses and small mansions of the Lowland country nobility (titled or untitled) which still stand preserved in one fashion or another and revealing in one way or another the centuries in which they were built or reached their climaxes, but revealing more consistently the spirit of Lowland Scottish architecture. White-harled, clean-lined, thick-walled, with a promise of deep comfort within, they rise out of partly moorland, partly cultivated landscapes as naturally and as sweetly as trees in full maturity rise from a glade.

Save in the Eastern Lowlands, where the influence of sandstone introduces a pervasive but not dominating note of faded pink amidst the darker colours, the architecture of the Lowlands is grey or white. There are none of those soft, sun-warmed, sun-mellowed shades of red brick or lemon yellow which illuminate and glow in the English scene. The grey is uncompromisingly and ineluctably grey; the white is purely and most satisfyingly white. Grey and white are the colours of austerity; and so, at its best as well as at its worst, Lowland Scottish architecture is austere. This note of severity is also to be seen even in the most modern buildings of the four great cities of Edinburgh, Glasgow, Dundee, and Aberdeen. But it is indubitably in the small town, the village, and in the rural architecture of the Lowlands that the true quality is seen and felt at its clearest.

Once again one has recourse to verse. And if it may seem odd to the stranger to our country that one should turn to poetry while discussing the allegedly unromantic Lowlands, while not referring to it at all when talking about the Highlands, it would not seem so to us. The very depth of feeling which the Lowlands have inspired amongst those who love them, the very fact that they often find it difficult to speak of it, often means that when this feeling does break out it is in the form of verse. Perhaps Stevenson in his celebrated poem about his well-loved Swanston Cottage has poetically exaggerated the high severity of the place, but he did, after all, call it *The House Beautiful*, and, having dwelt upon that severity, how richly he paints the contrast of its surroundings:

> Such is the place that I live in,
> Bleak without and bare within,
> Yet shall your ragged moor receive
> The incomparable pomp of eve,
> And the cold glories of the dawn
> Behind your shivering trees be drawn
> And when the wind from place to place
> Doth the unmoored cloud-galleons chase,
> Your garden gloom and gleam again,
> With leaping sun, with glancing rain.
> Here shall the wizard moon ascend
> The heavens, in the crimson end
> Of day's declining splendour. ...

The people who live in these Lowlands, whose lives have been shaped by this countryside and its history, who in their long traditions of their farming and building have to some extent shaped and influenced the land itself, are truly sons of their soil. They are severe in aspect, restrained in manner, serious in thought, and slow and measured in their expression of thought. At the same time they are full of deep feeling which is sometimes shown in a passionate and silent concentration of their energies, their spirit, and their intellects upon some task, some endeavour, great or small, or upon some intellectual exercise, philosophy, or religion. Sometimes, also, they reveal it in a passionate eloquence which, though it may startle the incomer, is no surprise to his fellow natives who are no more taken aback by it than they would be by 'the incomparable pomp of eve ... the crimson end of day's declining splendour', or 'the cold glories of the dawn' that regularly illuminate and colour Stevenson's (and their) moorland landscapes. Their emotional eloquence is sometimes poured out on religion, politics, or even philosophy. Sometimes, as in the anonymous Border ballads, it is nobly used for the purposes of imaginative narration. Sometimes, less nobly, but almost equally effectively, it lights up the telling of some ordinary story by an ordinary Scottish countryman or countrywoman. And sometimes its theme is love. In its narrative or amorous form, however, it is seldom sustained. The longest ballad, the most detailed Scottish country narrative, have their set limits; and the purest Scottish love poetry is lyric. Sometimes this Scottish eloquence can be tedious and over-expressed. Sometimes it is grossly sentimental. But at its best it is worthy of the Lowland scene at its most unexpectedly beautiful, and is deeply moving. Both in his long periods of restraint and in his rare moments of expressed emotion and of eloquence the Lowland Scot is a person who can touch the hearts of those who have learned to know him. He is also very courageous.

The less agreeable sides of his countryside and the more bitter parts of his history have affected him so that there is that in his manner, appearance, and perhaps even in his mentality which is repellent to or at least incomprehensible by the visitor from softer climates, from less arduous circumstances whose past has been less turbulent. The Lowlander has for centuries struggled to win a living from a soil that is not essentially unfruitful, but which has demanded from those who cultivate it every ounce of energy and capacity for enduring disappointment. The climate in which he has worked has been hard and capricious. Nature is always seeking to win back from him the land that he has conquered; and nature with him is often louring, threatening rather than beneficent. It is, too, more patently, more oppressively omnipresent in the shape of the great bare moorlands and hills which surround and hang over him than it is to the English countryman. In his aspect then, and his manner, he has acquired qualities from the land which is at once his support and his adversary. But he has had to put up with more than the land has had to endure, more than cruel winters, even crueller springs, sodden summers and autumns whose beneficence has come too late, more than wind, rain, and snow and frost.

He has had to endure the blows of man-made history as well as of geography and of weather. It is he who, for centuries, has had to meet and fend off the threats and the attempts at the foreign domination of Scotland. It was the Border and the South-East Lowlanders who were always the first to receive the invasion from England while the Highlanders were engaged upon their domestic disputes in the safer and remoter hills. All Scotland may have been stiffened, been welded into something like national unity by the blows of the Hammer of the Scots, Edward I, but it was on the Lowlanders that those blows fell first and hardest. It was the Lowlanders who for centuries after Wallace and Bruce had fought and won were in the first line of defence. In a sense they still are. Their countryside shows it. In their manner and their mentality they preserve the memory of it. For the most part of the life of our nation they have been the physical guardians of it; and something of the grimness of that guardianship remains about them still.

If it seems to the Englishman who has long ago forgotten the Anglo-Scottish wars somewhat far-fetched to attribute to their influence much in the manners and mind of the Lowlander, let him consider the case as it might have applied to his own country. Suppose that England had not been separated from the Continent. Suppose that she had with an heroic and bloody effort achieved her national unity and her national independence of a powerful, larger, and richer and contiguous France, suppose that independence to have been continually under threat until a little over two hundred years ago. And finally, suppose that London, like Edinburgh, had been only some fifty miles from the frontier – within easy marching distance from Calais. Having supposed all this, would it be surprising to find that the Southern English, and in particular those who lived in and guarded the land between London and the frontier (Kent, Surrey, Sussex, and Hampshire for distance), should have developed and sustained to this day the many characteristics derived from that centuries-old watchfulness, that centuries-old trial of endurance?

The less agreeable qualities which these hard circumstances and this hard history have given to the Lowlander are these. He is graceless and often irritatingly and depressingly suspicious of grace in others – though it must in justice be said that he is not in general a suspicious person. His celebrated laconic or taciturn manner has been the subject of much pawky and humorous writing,

ut it can verge upon downright rudeness, and can offend
he sensitive amongst his own race and nation as well as
disgust the foreigner. It is a manner of thought and expression which comes partly from deliberate restraint and
partly from shyness – a fear of giving himself away. It is
responsible for a depressing habit which he sometimes
displays to his disadvantage. Those who do not know him
would describe it as a continual and sour denigration.
But this would be unfair. He has a tendency, when faced
with anything new, to see and to point out the weakness
and the flaw in it right at the start, before he allows himself the luxury of praise. But this is not really a sour
railing (as his subsequent behaviour often shows); rather
it is a self-protective instinct. He feels that he must display his capacity for criticism at its sharpest before he
dare to discover his enthusiasm. Any writer, any artist,
any dreamer of dreams or schemer of schemes who ventures to put anything of himself before the Scottish
public must reconcile himself to these initial and depressing pinpricks from his compatriots or take his talents
elsewhere. He will reconcile himself in the knowledge
that if he is content to wait he will receive the balance of
praise, and the due praise of balanced criticism. He might
even win the accolade of 'no sae bad'.

He must remember that his compatriot's greatest fear is
of 'giving himself away'. The Lowland Scot is not, as he is
sometimes supposed to be, an ungenerous person. Nor,
indeed, in the end, is he anything but generous, even of
himself. If in the beginning 'himself' is that commodity
of which he is most careful, in the long run he is often the
most abandoned of all his company. This leads to the
reflection that his parsimony with himself at the beginning may be only based upon a principle of *bonne bouche*,

the saving of the tastiest morsel of a feast until the end. Or is this too fantastic? It would certainly be too fantastic a theory to put to him.

This side of the Scottish temperament, pushed to its most shocking extreme, is discovered in a story told in various forms of Lord Braxfield, the eighteenth-century Hanging Judge. Braxfield was a man of his age and kind, utterly opposed to reform. He was nonetheless, in matters of form at least, a religious man. He had in this version of the story been attending a service of his kirk at which a visiting minister had ventured to suggest that in certain circumstances and on certain matters there was something to be said for the principle of reform. After the sermon Braxfield encountered the offending divine in the precincts of the church, and, with his most judicial hanging look, gave him to understand that the sermon had not been to his taste. The poor minister, knowing that the Judge was a strong supporter of the Christian Faith, tried to defend himself by saying, 'You must remember, my Lord, that in his own day and time our Blessed Saviour was in some things accounted a Reformer.'

'Muckle guid He got o't', was his Lordship's appalling reply. 'He was haangit.'

There spoke, alas, a Lowland Scot in the full flood of his distaste for the principle of 'giving oneself away'. But who knows, who knows, when Lord Braxfield approached that ultimate *bonne bouche*, that last and tastiest morsel in the feast of life – Death – that he, too, may not have given himself away? Who knows that in the end he may not have cast back his fine Roman Scottish head upon the pillows and have ululated in a luxury of Lallans as he cried out and cast himself upon the merits and the mercy of Him who above all others gave Himself away?

There are, however, other things than reflexions of his awful nature that can mitigate the irritation one feels at this Lowland Scottish habit. There is, for instance, its occasional absurdity, an absurdity of exaggeration which is purely Scottish. The following incident, which is characteristic, really did happen – and quite recently too :–

A young couple had returned from a holiday with their families, bearing an album of enlarged snapshot photographs. They showed this to an elderly Scottish uncle who slowly and silently turned the pages over from beginning to end. Then equally slowly and with a larger deliberation he turned them back again, examining each one until he came once more to the beginning. Finally he picked upon one picture and, after a short deliberation, pointed to it. 'That's the worst.'

While the Lowland Scot's hospitality at home is proverbial, abroad he seems to take a particular pleasure in airing his gracelessness, and is grossly censorious of the manners, habits, and beliefs of the strangers amongst whom he finds himself. In this he thinks he is striking a rigidly national attitude. In fact, he succeeds only in giving an undeserved impression of provinciality, which is distressing and shameful to other Scots in whose company he may find himself, and is laughable to strangers. He is inclined to intemperance both in indulgence and in abstinence. His drinking is not a gay affair, and his teetotalism is severe and arrogant. He is highly amorous, but, save for those miraculous moments when some innate tenderness breaks out in the lyrics of his language, his lovemaking is crude and to the point. And yet, so incalculable is the female sex, it is often more successful than the more polished amorist would believe. He is clannish and has the clansman's respect for gentle birth, but is often careful to conceal it, implying in his manner to the more fortunately born that he is as good as they are. In this he differs from the Highlander whose equally strong clannishness makes him more politely prefer to give the impression that they may be as good as he is. His appearance is often unnecessarily and intensely lugubrious; and the sight of a row of unsmiling Lowland faces in a train, a country bus, or at the bar of the village inn can be very depressing. Ah, but the kindliness of them when they do smile!

On that note the present chronicler really must bring to an end this list of his Lowland compatriot's failings of address and mentality. Let it be enough to say two things. First, these failings are much less obvious in the women than in the men of Scotland. Second, though this list of his depressing habits could be lengthened still further, all these and other failings are, for those who really know him, compensated for by three virtues of manner, character, and of the spirit which he often possesses quite as largely as his failings – his dignity, his kindliness, and the paradox of his deep poetic feeling, a feeling strangely enough that can exist in him quite unaffected by his gracelessness and his distrust of grace.

Gracelessness and kindliness, poetic feeling and taciturnity. These, however, are not the qualities for which he is most famed in the outer world. There, let it be admitted, he is usually supposed (sometimes with humorous affection) to be both mean in money matters and incapable of seeing a joke. The innumerable pleasantries of which he has been the subject on these scores have become a part not only of British but of international tradition – for it is the Lowlander rather than the Scot in general who is the real source of all the 'Scotch jokes' in the world.

Of course, the jokes have a basis in fact; of course, the Lowland Scot is by certain standards (to put it mildly) careful of his money and humourless. By other standards he is the reverse. He has so often been defended from these imputations by genial and generous-minded English visitors who have enjoyed his hospitality that it would be unnecessary and laboured for a compatriot to repeat their kind remarks. This, however, may be said.

Throughout her existence Scotland has been a poor country; and poverty has fallen particularly harshly on the Lowlander. He is therefore painfully conscious of the value of small pieces of money. On the other hand, his pride in hospitality will not allow him to count the cost when he is entertaining a guest. Pride also makes it distasteful for him to discuss money matters; and by paradox he is thus often lured into extravagances in sums that are (to him at least) large. The history of Scotland is full of incidents when the Scot has thrown his all into wild and extravagant schemes with a passion which would be quite foreign to the Englishman. In general, it may be said that the Lowland Scot is generous and (on occasions) abandoned in big things, and comically careful in small matters.

The Scottish sense of humour is another matter. There is no need to defend it against the English conception of 'the funny'; it is simply that it is a different brand. It has often been called 'dry' – though whether this means that the English form is 'wet' is not clear. Much of Lowland Scottish humour depends upon grotesque under- or sometimes over-statement delivered with an unsmiling face. Nor do its practitioners demand the sudden guffaw of satisfaction from their audience, which makes, if one is in the mood for it, the telling of a successful humorous story so amiable an experience in England. Instead, the Scottish humourist prefers to watch the effect of his art slowly and warmly growing and glowing amongst those who listen to him in the form of delayed chuckles, smiles, or sometimes mere expressionless movements of the body. It is thus also that the traditional Lowland Scot prefers to receive his humour. He likes to taste it on the tongue of his mind and roll it round the mouth of his imagination, to savour it in fact rather than to swallow it noisily. Both forms of making and receiving humour have their merits, and it is unprofitable to compare them. At the same time it might surprise some English people to learn that many people in Scotland genuinely and without affectation look upon the English as lacking in a true sense of humour.

Lowland caution and Lowland 'pawky humour' have been the subject of nearly all the stock Scotch jokes of the last fifty years. But if we Scots, whether Highland or Lowland, find the laboured repetition of them sometimes a trifle irritating, we have to admit that it is we, or at least some of our celebrated ones, who have done most to propagate the legends. The late Sir Harry Lauder was in his own kind an artist of the first class, but it was his world-wide popularity that spread the notion of Scottish meanness all over the world. Is it humourless and hypersensitive to point this out? Perhaps it is. But let the Englishman for a moment ponder on what he would think of an English comedian of genius whose rich talents spread through the entire globe a notion of the English based on their less amiable characteristics – insensitivity, ruthlessness, blindness to beauty, or (in the good old days) gross over-eating.

The partly sentimental, partly ridiculous legend of the pawky Scot has, too, been much helped by some of our more popular writers at the end of the last century and the beginning of this one. They, too, in their way were men and women of talent; but their talents have had for us Scots some unfortunate results. It is not only that they have disseminated a crude stock view of us, but that they have been directly responsible for the behaviour of some of our more embarrassing Scottish public figures in England and further abroad. Those of us who have sat hotly blushing while listening to a 'heid o' depairtment' in London 'doing his stuff' at a board meeting or at a staff gathering, who have heard in painful silence the club Scotch pawky bore (possibly slightly tight) holding forth by the club fireside know well upon what fictional characters these compatriots of ours are modelling themselves.

But to belabour the poor Kailyarders for their well-meant and often skilful literary efforts would be at this date absurd. They are not much read now; though it is unfortunate that they should have helped to set up a type which even now some Scots feel obliged to imitate. Should the reader wish to find the true Lowland Scottish character in our literature he will discover him in abundance and in great variety in Scott, Stevenson, and in that charming little classic *Reminiscences of Scottish Life and Character* by Dean Ramsay, in Galt's *Annals of the Parish*, and other earlier nineteenth-century works. These are, it is true, writers from the past. But, they had the advantage of writing before the 'Scotch legend' set in at its hardest. Moreover, it cannot be too firmly stressed that the characters which they described on which they chose as models live on in their descendants in the Lowlands of

Scotland to-day. Anyone who has been to Ireland knows that the Irish peasant has effortlessly survived in his true character despite all the Begorrah-bejabbers-Ould Ireland efforts of the professional sentimentalists and humorists when Ireland was still considered by English (and alas! some Irish) writers to be a fit subject only for humour and sentimentality. It is perhaps not so generally known that the true Scottish Lowlander in his true character has also survived the efforts of his own particular brand of sentimentalists and humorists to make him conform to the models of their fertile imaginations.

But the Scottish Lowlander has survived more than this sort of thing. Indeed an obstinate and vigorous power of survival is one of the most obvious elements in him. He appears to relish the difficulties with which he has to contend in order to make his character and his kind live on. There is something like a grim gusto in the manner in which he retains his habits of life, of speech, and of thought in the face of changing and often adverse circumstances. In his Southern and Eastern marches he acted for centuries as the guardian of Scotland against the ceaseless encroachment of a powerful Southern neighbour. And to-day, though he has no longer any need to defend Scotland by arms within the island of Great Britain, he is grimly, yet at the same time without self-consciousness, set upon defending her nationality in civil matters. It is due to the Border Lowlander's deeply implanted conservatism, his tenacity in custom of thought and expression, that the traveller from England, as soon as he crosses the Border, feels not that he is merely going northwards but is entering a new nation. The transition at Berwick or at Carter Bar is not gradual but abrupt, and none but the most insensitive could fail to notice it.

In the North and East, in Fife, in Angus, Aberdeen-shire, and in the final projection of his country, the land of Buchan, he has scarcely any ancestral memories of attack from the enemies of Scotland furth of Scotland. But here, too, he has discovered his gusto for survival against constant adversity. With the mysterious wild Cel-tic hinterland of the Highlands behind and above him, with the grey North Sea constantly battering his shores, he has stuck to his soil and his background with an astonish-ing and fruitful fortitude. He has, too, retained here his Lowland Scottish habits of mind and custom and speech with a vigorous tenacity which has defied more success-fully than anywhere else in the country the levelling and unifying influences of our age – the cinema, the wireless, and quick transport.

This capacity for survival, this deep durability of the Lowlander has had a great effect on the whole Scottish nation, and on the effect that nation has made on the world. The more fluent, more obviously romantic, more easily attractive, and (by reason of emigration) more travelled or dispersed Celtic Highlander may have carried a certain picturesque notion of the Scot to the Dominions and across the Atlantic, but it is by the qualities of the Lowlander that Scotland is for the most part known in Great Britain and in Europe. It is his austerity, his application, his taciturnity, his courage and, alas! his gracelessness that have impressed a par-ticular notion of the Scot upon much of the outside world. And (and this is an important fact which should never be forgotten by any Scot, Highland or Lowland) it is his poetry that has caught the ear of the world and has given it most forcibly the other, the unexpected side of the Scot. It is from the Lowlands that there came the anonymous and deathless Border Ballads, the lyrics of Burns, and the romances of Walter Scott.

So he survives, endures, and impresses, and is likely to continue to do so for a long time. For the most part of a millennium he has survived the weather, the poverty of his land, and the English. He is unlikely to give in easily now.

CHAPTER FOUR

THE TWO CITIES

IT is only forty miles from Edinburgh to Glasgow. Either by road or by one of the frequent trains it will not take you much more than an hour to travel between the two cities. You can do this several times a day if you feel so inclined; and a number of business men live in Edinburgh and go to their work in Glasgow. There are even some who do the reverse, sleeping in Glasgow and working in Edinburgh. There are also people whose work is evenly divided between the two and who have homes in each city.

The forty-mile belt that connects the two chief towns of Scotland passes through an on the whole dull landscape, undivided by hills, minor watersheds or rivers or any recognizable natural breaks. Scattered indeterminately upon its length are small towns and villages, most of them of nineteenth-century industrial or mining growth. There is not very much difference between them; for they are all products of the Glasgow-Edinburgh belt, and not of either city. Near Glasgow they become a little more conglomerate and grim. Nearer Edinburgh they lie about more starkly and individually scattered. It is difficult to tell, however, where the Eastern Scotland influence ends and the Western begins. Nor is it likely that anyone, save the most curious, has tried to discover. The journey by road or rail is too quick and too dull to merit much investigation or even attention.

And yet, the journey having been made, and having

arrived in Glasgow from Edinburgh or in the Capital of Scotland from the great city of the West, one does not need to be curious or unusually observant to notice that one has passed from one world into another. All within the small country of Scotland and merely by travelling an easy forty miles. The differences between these two worlds are those of character, of East and West, of climate and appearance, but most of all of character.

The character of Edinburgh and the character of Glasgow, so vivid, so complementary to each other, are in their roots as Scottish as the characters of the Highlands and the Lowlands. For nearly a century and a half they have been as important in the general pattern of the character of Scotland as even the Highlands and the Lowlands were. It is impossible to know the Scotland of to-day without savouring the difference between the quality of Edinburgh and of Glasgow – and this is not because they are the two largest and most important towns in Scotland : it is because the difference between them is of the essence of Scotland.

The differences in the characters of the two cities may have been slightly influenced by climate and geography, but far the greatest factor in their great diversity has lain in history. Each city is most strikingly and, even for European cities, unusually shaped and influenced by its past. To this day each is strongly conscious of this and proclaims it in its way of life. Any perceptive visitor, even if he stays but for a short time, becomes aware of this, as much in the bustling modern Glasgow as in the more obviously historic Capital of Scotland.

It is a thousand years since the first houses began to huddle beneath the protection of Edinburgh Castle Rock and to form themselves into a conscious unit. It is not much less than a thousand years since that unit, under the name of Edinburgh, began to be the most important Scottish town; and it is over six hundred years since it became the official and recognized Capital, the seat of the Court and the Government. Since then Edinburgh's growth has been the scene of violent intrigue in high places and much bloody action amongst kings and nobles; she has had her periods of prosperity and international fame, alternating with those of neglect and decay, but she has as a city throughout the centuries grown on the whole easily and with confidence. She has grown by slow design and by deliberate effort, striking her roots deeper with every expansion. She has never swollen to an unmanageable size and has always remained a conscious unit.

As the capital of a small but independent northern country with alliances abroad, she continued to brave the vicissitudes of international politics as well as the winds and tempests that yearly howled about her in her rock-perched position. Then in 1707, with the loss of her Parliament at the Union, she received the severest blow since her life as a capital. For a few years men thought that she had lost her position and would sink to being no more than a county town. In a short time, however, she recovered in an astonishing way and began that period which some still to-day look upon as her golden age – the second half of the eighteenth century.

In the nineteenth century she lost this proud international position, but her place in Scotland was now assured, founded again, impregnable and imperturbable. There were some who during this period found her imperturbable conservatism and frigid self-assurance irritating and did not hesitate to say so. They could not, however, challenge her easy assumption of leadership in

Scotland. She was the centre of all the indigenous Scottish institutions left to Scotland, her legal system, and her Kirk. Moreover, her roots struck deep into the past of Scotland as Scotland's Capital. Scotland knew it and recognized it. What is perhaps more important is that Edinburgh herself knew it and accepted it. From this assured position at the turn of the century she grew to her present state – one in which she has more actual and vital claims to leadership than even she had in the immediate past.

Glasgow's past is, in matter of time, in number of years, as long as Edinburgh's, but it has been very different. The Glasgow that we know to-day did not begin to exist until two hundred years ago, nor did it reach the proportion, the shape, and the style with which we are familiar until the time when our grandfathers were children. Before that metamorphosis which suddenly thrust modern Glasgow darkly, forcibly, insistently, and overpoweringly into the consciousness of Scotland and the Western world, this city of the West was for centuries a completely different place.

It was a small Cathedral and University town upon the banks of a pellucid trout and salmon stream that wandered shallowly and innocently between orchard and Lowland fields and was not navigable save by the smallest boats. Its history in this *rôle* was ancient and it prided itself on being the oldest town in Scotland. It has in that long, lasting, pristine state often been likened to St Andrews, which to this day glimmers like a lonely star from that forgotten Scotland upon the isolation of the promontory of the East Neuk of Fife and amidst the wash, upon three sides, of the grey North Sea. Even so, like a lonely star (for Glasgow was then in an isolated part of Scotland), the Glasgow of the old ecclesiastical and learned times glimmered on its own in the West, not upon a promontory in the sea, but under the looming presence of the then just as mysterious Highland hills.

The event which began the transformation of this minuscule Scottish Oxford into a Scottish Manchester and Liverpool combined was a political one, the Union of the Scottish and English Parliaments in 1707. This Act, which delivered such a severe blow to the pride and position of Edinburgh, which even threatened her existence as a capital, quickly conferred commercial blessings on Glasgow. The Glasgow merchants may have, in common with other Scotsmen, felt a humiliation at the loss of Scottish independence; but it was a pain that was soon assuaged by the consciousness of filling coffers and bulging pockets in their city of the West.

Until 1707 Scotland had been forbidden trade with the English Colonies – that is to say, with most of the New World across the Atlantic. After the Union of Parliaments this restriction on Scottish shipping and Scottish merchants was removed. The Golden West was now open to Scotland; and the gateway to it was Scotland's great western river, the Clyde. Glasgow, as the city of the Clyde, at once felt the advantage of this, and at once and energetically took that advantage. It was to the New World that Europe looked for all her tobacco and nearly all her sugar; and it was not long before Glasgow became, as the entrance through which these increasingly desired goods came to Europe, not only the most important port in Scotland, but one of the most influential in Great Britain and Europe.

This new-found prosperity endured some set-backs, the most grievous of which was the loss of the American

81

Colonies after the War of Independence, but Glasgow was now set upon a course from which she could not be deflected. She turned her now-urgent energies into the fostering of many other commercial undertakings for which her position in Scotland and in the West of Europe fitted her. These were many and diverse; and when the Napoleonic Wars were over and the nineteenth century was in its third decade Glasgow had begun to take the large shape and assume the vivid, vital, romantic, expanding, inquisitive, and acquisitive character which has made her famous for over a century. The transformation which had begun a hundred years earlier, soon after the Union of the Parliaments, was by the 1830's and 1840's complete. And though in the rest of the century Glasgow grew in fortune and in size, suffered reverses and recovered from them again, she retained and indeed enforced the character she then acquired. Despite many twentieth-century changes and twentieth-century vicissitudes in fortune she retains it to the present day. In this brief paragraph is summed up a history of Glasgow's industrial development, which will be dealt with at greater length in the chapter on industry.

The differences between this new Glasgow and the triumphantly surviving Edinburgh have been so keenly and so personally felt by the inhabitants that even now, after only a little more than a century, they seem to have become traditional. Perhaps it is the more vocal, the more self-sensitive Glaswegians who are most aware of them, who speak most of them. At any rate it is they who speak most eloquently of their differences from their near neighbour.

In the present writer's hearing a Glasgow girl once described her regular returns from the neighbourhood of

Edinburgh to Glasgow and the West with an enthusiasm which was as eloquent as that which you might hear from an exile coming home across the Atlantic. She worked upon an East Lothian farm, and once a month went home to her parents' house on the outskirts of Glasgow and on the Firth of Clyde. In making this journey she not only went from the most characteristic East of Scotland scenery to the most characteristic part of the West, she also had to pass through and linger for a while in both Edinburgh and Glasgow.

She described how, on the Saturday of her week-end holiday, she would leave the wide, austere, cold, yet agriculturally fertile country of East Lothian with its houses of pink stone seeming to cower squatly in the wide landscape so open to the east winds. When she arrived in Edinburgh she did not deny that the precipitous beauty of the ancient City with its Castle-crowned rock and its wide eighteenth-century expansiveness always impressed her, and in any weather, for she was a lass of sensibility. But Scottish though she was, and though this was the Capital of her country, she could not feel at home in it. Not for her these steep and windy heights, these 'hanging gardens of the New Town', these massive squares, octagons, crescents, and streets with the hidden and contrasting byways slinking behind them. Nor was she moved to anything but an objective and even irritated admiration of the human contrast between what seemed to her the stiff rectitude of the strollers in Princes Street and the coarser crowds in the Old Town. It was all very picturesque, but very strange and foreign (an epithet often applied to Edinburgh by other than Glasgow or West Country folk) ; indeed, she once made the shocking statement that she felt less estranged in the Capital of England than in the Capital of Scotland. One did not approve, but one saw what she meant.

Then she would, with a sense of relief, take the afternoon train to Glasgow. It was the winter homecomings that she remembered most clearly and spoke of most vividly. She would emerge by the side entrance from the Central Station in Glasgow into the lamplit clamour of Argyle Street. She could easily have made her first contact with the streets of Glasgow through the more conventional front way out at the corner of Hope Street. But no, she preferred to taste at once and as quickly as possible the full tang of the change between the East where she had been exiled and the West where she had been born. It was with a real Scotch emotional gusto that she would describe the swarming Saturday-afternoon crowds underneath 'the Highlandman's Umbrella' (the railway bridge over Argyle Street), shouting, laughing, jostling, and talking in sing-song *argot* of Glasgow that was music to her ears, the ceaseless clangour of the tramcars, the gleam of lighted shop windows in the mud, the clatter of the great Clydesdale dray horses' hooves upon the cobble stones, and faintly above, or faintly penetrating through the multifarious din, the sound of a ship's siren coming in from the fog of the nearby Clyde. How vivid everything was! How vital everyone was, and how unself-conscious they were! This was life, and the teeming life of her own city of Glasgow at its most vital, on a Saturday afternoon. For a few minutes she would allow herself the pleasure of wandering and looking and listening and relishing. Then she would take the train to her home further down the river where it widens out into the Firth, and into the West, but somehow never quite leaving behind it the feel of Glasgow. 'To go from the East of Scotland to the West on a Saturday afternoon,' she would say, 'is like travelling between England and France; and there is as much difference between Edinburgh and Glasgow as between Dover and Calais.'

She was right, or very nearly right, and most Edinburgh civic patriots would certainly agree with her. If it is the recollection of her enthusiasm that has been called upon to illustrate this sense of difference between Glasgow and Edinburgh, it should not be supposed that there are not amongst Edinburgh exiles in the West those who could be equally lyrical about returning to their own city across this gulf of forty miles. Indeed, there is one who remembers very well a two-year enforced sojourn in Glasgow some time ago. There was much that he learned to admire and like and be excited about in Glasgow during those two years, but the recollections of the purest pleasure that come back to him from that period are those of his own all-too-infrequent escapes to Edinburgh from the West. He can recall with a fervour equal to that of the Glasgow girl on her returns to Glasgow how he would emerge after long intervals from the Waverley Station in Edinburgh and would breathe again with gratitude the wide and spacious beauty of his own town, and would encounter again, as if it were something new, the slow, formal, and kindly manners of its inhabitants, his own fellow-citizens.

This almost personal sense of difference between Edinburgh and Glasgow is most keenly felt by the citizens of Scotland's two greatest cities – sometimes too keenly. And it is for someone who admires the qualities, as well as recognizes the faults, of both places, however much his loyalties and likings are tied to one, often irritating to observe the sharpness of the rivalry that exists between them. It is true that that rivalry for the most part is confined to small matters, and that when any major threat to Scotland or to the prickly sense of Scottish independence arises, the rivalry disappears in a profounder sense of common Scottish nationality. The gulf, then, of forty miles (small geographically, and enormously wide in other ways) closes with the snap of a pair of jaws in an angry face. Still, apart from these times of outside threat or pressure the rivalry exists, constant, and foolish. It is foolish for two reasons. First, neither city could ever replace or overcome the other in what each is best at. Second, it would be difficult to find elsewhere in Europe two cities so near to each other, so rooted in their national soil and character, yet so different and at the same time so nearly perfectly complementary. This surely, in a small, highly individualistic country such as Scotland, should be looked upon as a stroke of luck, or, better still, as a matter for pride and pleasure and not as a source of mutual irritation.

For they are indeed complementary. Edinburgh is old – amongst the oldest cities of Northern Europe – yet she often surprises her sister of forty miles away by an unexpected sprightly old-lady-like capacity for seizing the opportune moment and being nearly in advance of the times. The Edinburgh Festival was a case in point. Glasgow is for the most part new, and is even yet the urgent, vital child of the Industrial Revolution. Yet she, too, has an unexpected devotion to the past which is not only a romantic love for something she largely lacks; it also arises from the fact that she has, deeply overlaid by her large and immediate nineteenth-century past, the foundations of a past almost as old as is Edinburgh's.

People are apt to forget this; and Glasgow folk are always, and rightly, eager to remind you of it. Thus in matters of time and of history Edinburgh and Glasgow are neatly and precisely complementary.

Glasgow, with her muddy golden sunsets, her muddy golden stream, her ramshackle and aspiring but never wholly successful building, is essentially and in appearance a romantic city. Edinburgh, with her small spaciousness, her contained steepness, is not, as she has been poetically spoken of, 'mine own romantic town', but rather our own classical city. For all that, she has romantic decorations about her and within her, as, in a like manner of contrast, Glasgow, for all her romantic sprawling, has a strong and sometimes overpowering veneer of realism. Thus the two cities are again complementary.

Edinburgh is austere, old, and at root unshockable, as are all old and historic places that have learned in the process of the centuries that some things in human nature are incurable – and, on the whole, perhaps just as well uncured. Glasgow is not austere, but is rather naïvely abandoned in her morality and her immorality, in her respectability, and in her disrepute. Her vivid slum life, with its gang warfare and its pseudo-American native journalists preying upon the so-called picturesque elements in that life, is very obviously wicked – Edinburgh's low life is less obviously low, but is probably more profound. It is certainly more historic. Edinburgh's respectability, on the other hand, is more easily apparent than is the equivalent side of Glasgow, but it is in reality not nearly so hidebound, so fearful of its position. Nothing in Edinburgh is so 'respectable' as is the upper crust of Glasgow, floating uneasily upon a turbulent sea of Glasgow-Irish disreputability. In this naïve naughtiness and this austere unshockability, Glasgow and Edinburgh are again complementary.

Glasgow's great river of Clyde rises amidst the moorland hills far from Glasgow and pushes its way through the muddy city and the clanging shipyards out into the Atlantic and to the furthest parts of the Earth. Thus Glasgow's dreams for Scotland, of which she is the chief port, are of transatlantic and remote places. Edinburgh's small stream, the Water of Leith, begins but a small distance outside the town and chatters its way by and through part of it into the Firth of Forth, which wholly passes Edinburgh by. That Firth of Forth is Edinburgh's gateway to the outer world; but it is a gateway that leads only to Europe. Herein lies one of the most significant of the complementary differences between the Capital of Scotland and her larger and more modern sister. Historically and geographically Edinburgh is linked with the civilization of Europe. Glasgow's aspirations are towards the New World; and the foundations of her prosperity have lain there. In this respect their backs are turned upon each other, yet their feet are firmly placed upon Scottish soil; and their roots are in the Scottish past.

Glasgow's climate is moist and soft, and her humid atmosphere is full of the smoke of industry. Edinburgh is, if not exactly a dry place, full of cleansing, bracing (sometimes over-bracing) air; and her rainstorms are great sweeping things that violently wash the city and do not drizzle on her. Edinburgh is, of course, the more beautiful city; but, as has been said, Glasgow is the more romantic and is surrounded by scenery more beautiful and more romantic than Edinburgh's. She has a kind of near-hinterland of the Highlands and of the sea coast West Highlands in her Loch Lomond district and in her unsurpassed estuary of the Clyde. And yet, any true lover of Edinburgh who has been exiled for any length of time in Glasgow and the West finds himself at length longing for the wide plains of the Lothians, his own Pentland Hills, standing right by his city's gates, the grey North Sea, the grey coast of Fife opposite, and the sense of space and freedom that is particularly Edinburgh's.

Glasgow is a city of commerce, Edinburgh of the professions. Glasgow, both by reason of her commercial background and because of something temperamental in her, is volatile and subject to booms and slumps in prosperity and in mood. One of Edinburgh's chief characteristics is her magnificent imperturbability. Glasgow is quick to enthusiasm and quick to anger, and sometimes violent in obstruction as well as in action. Edinburgh is not: her feelings are deep and move her slowly but none the less surely than Glasgow moves. Glasgow, as the interviews of celebrated visitors by her journalists show, longs to be liked – and often is. Edinburgh certainly likes to be liked and admired, but is almost impervious to abuse: she is sure of herself. Glasgow is by far the richer city: Edinburgh is indubitably the Capital.

All these complementary differences between Edinburgh and Glasgow have had, of course, their obvious effects upon the people who live in these cities forty miles apart. It is impossible to move about the streets, pubs, cafés, and tea shops of Glasgow for little more than a week without realizing that this is one of the most warmhearted cities in Europe; and with the true (but now alas! disappearing) London side of London the most warmhearted in Britain.

Indeed, the 'working class' Glaswegian has many qualities in common with the true Cockney. He is humorous, self-reliant, and self-sufficient, and often has an odd Scottish equivalent of the Cockney's perkiness. Like the Cockney he is very fond of enjoying himself on high days and holidays, going about in droves of his own kind with much display of colour and music. He is, however, more emotional or sentimental, as you will, than the Cockney, and this shows itself in many ways, not least when he is on a holiday jaunt. An expedition 'Doon the Watter' (a trip on one of the pleasure steamers in the estuary of the Clyde on a Fair holiday) may at times remind you of certain elements in a Hampstead Heath bank holiday, but by the end of the day a quite unCockney, indeed unEnglish, note has crept in – an agreeably sentimental melancholy. It will not be shared by all (for to the end of the day there will always be vociferous and humorous groups round the ship's bar) but it is easily perceptible. As the little ship turns home again from its voyage through the extravagant beauties of Glasgow's own Firth of Clyde you will notice that the crowds seem to begin to be affected by the scene and the occasion – the holiday's end. There is less jauntiness, less loud speaking and laughter. And the ship's band, quick to catch the prevailing mood, will strike up the well-remembered sentimental ditties which have outlasted the decades, 'Roamin' in the Gloamin'', 'I Love a Lassie', and 'Loch Lomond'. Nor will it do to dismiss this as only the easy sentimentality of an exhausted holiday crowd. There is more to it than that. Something in the temperament of these Glasgow holiday makers has responded to the sea and the hills, and the colours and the smaller and more domestic beauties of Glasgow's and their own particular pleasure and water garden, the Firth of Clyde. They are moved and touched and made pleasantly sad by the patent loveliness which they have enjoyed on their annual outing. And perhaps too in their hearts they are a little proud, proud of the beauties of what they, who have not yet learned to become sophisticated, would not be ashamed to call 'Bonnie Scotland'.

That something in their temperament that makes them respond to the beauty that has lain about them on their holiday trip comes partly from a general Scottish capacity for emotion. It also comes from the strong admixture of Celtic blood that is to be found in Glasgow. Inverness may be 'the Capital of the Highlands' but Glasgow is the Highland Capital of Great Britain. There are certainly more Highlanders, both those consciously Highland and Gaelic-speaking and those whose connexion with the North is not quite so immediate, than in any other town in Scotland or England. They permeate every part of Glasgow life; and it is partly their blood that is responsible for the quickness and the gaiety of the Glasgow crowds. It is their blood too which, mixed with the essential Lowland blood of Glasgow, gives the Glaswegian an occasional and unexpected sad grimness which the Cockney never has.

But there is another and strong Celtic element in Glasgow which has been the cause of much controversy and still is. Mr C. A. Oakley in his book *The Second City* says: 'There is no subject on which writers and speakers about Glasgow are less willing to dwell than that of the Irish in Scotland.' This is certainly true; for it is a subject on which Glasgow folk are usually either vociferous (on either side) or markedly silent. Any writer on Scotland then who does not come from Glasgow must be wary when talking about the Irish in Glasgow. Nevertheless it is a subject which must be mentioned, even in a general essay of this kind, for it is impossible to consider Glasgow of the mid twentieth century without considering the Irish in Glasgow.

When Glasgow was at the start of her nineteenth-century prosperity she attracted a certain number of poor Irish immigrants who were ready to undertake the meanest industrial work at low wages. At first Glasgow, with her quickly growing industries, was able to absorb these incomers without the resentment of her own indigenous population. In the 1840's however the position changed. The appalling Irish famine which reached its climax in 1846 threw out upon the world a pathetic mass of starving Irish peasants ready and willing to undertake any kind of work in order to live. Some of these found their way to America, others to England, but the majority took the easiest and shortest route out of Ireland by the Northern Irish Sea to Glasgow.

The arrival and the continued stream of these immigrants at once created a problem which, according to the Glasgow authorities, is not settled yet. The Irish became unpopular with Glasgow Scots and in particular with the Lowlanders on account of their readiness to accept low wages for almost any work. They were accused also of lowering the already miserable standard of living in the quarters of the city where they established themselves. The introduction too of large numbers of poverty-stricken but faithful Catholics created problems of its own kind in what had been until then the politically Whiggish and religiously Protestant city of Glasgow. Nor was it only the Catholic Irish who created problems. The Ulster immigrants brought their own religious warfare with them which they continued to wage in the poorer streets of Glasgow with their Catholic compatriots. The Glasgow gang warfare for which the city is still, perhaps exaggeratedly, notorious has its origins in this now century-old segregation of the Irish into rival groups.

The problem remains. The Irish have now for more than three generations settled down in Glasgow, and have since the establishment of the Irish Republic become British citizens. They are accused by those who resent their presence in Glasgow and Scotland of divided loyalties, of an ineradicable taste for squalor, which does much to perpetuate the worst Glasgow slums, of a tendency to convivial violence which though confined mostly to attacks on their own kind keep the Glasgow police busy and lower the general standard of morality in the city. Though of the same racial strain as some Scots, they are often accused of being 'dirty half foreigners'. Their habit of marrying amongst themselves and begetting large families is also implicitly rather than explicitly resented. Glasgow feels she cannot assimilate them and feels uncomfortable about it.

On the other hand, the Irish with their long memories ask, with some justification, whose fault it is that the present situation has arisen. They deny that they have divided loyalties, and ask why it should be considered disloyal to retain an affection for the land of their ancestry, and above all to cling to the faith of their fathers. They accuse their usually better off and better placed Glasgow Scottish critics of bigotry, intolerance, and short-sightedness; for, as their more vocal supporters are quick to point out, the presence of a large number of Catholics in the poorer quarters of Glasgow is a sure antidote against Communism.

The problem remains; and only a Glasgow writer or critic should dare to suggest a solution. This, however, can be said objectively. Glasgow may not be able to assimilate the Celtic Irish in the way that she has assimilated the Celtic Scots from the Highlands, but to the outside observer the Irish element has helped to make the Glasgow character and has contributed to it some of those qualities which we admire in it. Would the Glasgow liveliness and vitality be quite so lively and vital without the admixture of Irish blood? Would the celebrated 'Glesca' type which is the joy of music hall audiences, and the repetition of whose terse and witty sayings fills so many columns of the Glasgow press, be quite so much himself without that faint but pervasive touch of Irishness in his speech and manner? And finally, has not the Irish element contributed largely to the reputation of the Glasgow soldier in warfare of which Glasgow is justly proud? It is possible that the Irish cannot be assimilated into the body of Glasgow, but they have become so much a part of the pattern of Glasgow that they have, to the outside observer at least, permanently affected the character of the place and in so doing have contributed to the immense vitality of the Celtic Capital of Britain and the umquhile second city of the Empire.

Glasgow is volatile, a city of change and motion. It is only in the last century that she attained her immense position. Change and motion, therefore, is in the minds of everyone, even amongst her richest and apparently placidly prosperous citizens, many of whom can remember grandfathers or fathers who by reason of Glasgow's capacity for change and motion rose from the humblest circumstances. It is perhaps the knowledge of this in their past, and the fear that change and motion may work upon them in the reverse direction, that makes the Glasgow ruling classes so tenaciously respectable. If in her poorer population Glasgow is the Celtic Capital of Britain she is in her upper crust the most Whiggish town in Britain.

Glasgow's memorable murder trial, that of Madeleine Smith in the 1850's, has many fascinating facets for the student of life as well as for the criminologist. Not the least of these is the fact that the whole drama of poison and illicit love was played out on the stage of Glasgow upper middle class respectability. What appalled our forefathers of ninety years ago was not the thought that a young girl might have poisoned her lover (and got off on a Not Proven verdict) but the undoubted fact that that apparently sweet young girl should have come from the very cream of the rising Victorian Glasgow society and should have had as her admitted lover a squalid young foreigner of a disreputable kind. One can still feel the faint tremor of the shock they must have felt as the sordid details came out in court for the first time. In all Britain only Glasgow's upper middle class could have provided a setting of such dramatic contrast for such a tale.

But it is in between this uneasily floating crust of respectability and the moving tide of the poorer classes that the effects of change and motion in Glasgow life are most potent. The flux and flow of curiosity and adventure in matters of the mind, in literature, in art, in politics for which Glasgow has been noted not only in Scotland but far further afield takes place for the most part in the intermediate and freer world between poverty and wealth.

It is amongst the schoolteachers, the students, the younger medical men, the journalists, the actors, the artists, and the fairly insecurely and moderately paid groups of workers in Glasgow that there has long fermented that inquisitiveness, that eagerness for experiment, that intelligent discontent which has gained for Glasgow the name of being the most intellectually alive town in Scotland. It is a reputation which nowadays Glasgow may find a little difficulty in sustaining; for of recent years it has been in the East and in the North that the most vigorous manifestations of Scottish intellectual vitality have taken place. Still it is a reputation founded on a very active past which is by no means dead. It is no longer ago than the turn of the century that the Glasgow School of painting was making the name of the city famous in the art world of Europe. At the same time Charles Rennie Mackintosh was in Glasgow laying the foundations of the modern school of architecture. And fifty years ago too it was in Glasgow that men of science, philosophy, and politics were dreaming new dreams that they were later to see becoming actual. And it was in the intermediate and uncertain classes of Glasgow that nearly all this intellectual activity took place. Nowadays, with the strong animal vitality of the great city somewhat less pronounced, this activity is not quite so obvious, so wide in its influence. But it persists and exists, and among the same kind of people.

Is there a Glasgow type, a Sam Weller, a Mr Pickwick, or a Marius of the Clyde? There are various candidates, various Glasgow 'characters' in fiction who have caught the imagination of the public. J. J. Bell's Wee MacGregor and his family, Private Spud Tamson, the Gorbals diehards; their patron and protector Dickson McCunn in the John Buchan thrillers, in more modern times, and in the modern manner of the wireless, the McFlannels, but greatest of all and by far the most memorable that Glasgow creation of an Edinburgh magician, Walter Scott's Bailie Nicol Jarvie. Having mentioned that unforgettable figure from the novel of *Rob Roy*, what about Rob Roy himself? He may have been a Highland free-booter who lived both in fact and in fiction over two hundred years ago, but if he can be said to have influenced any Scottish town it was not Inverness or Inverary but Glasgow – the Glasgow in which at night time the Bailie heard 'thae Hielan deevils whooing and whustling' in the dark. Yes, Rob Roy and his kind have left a strain of their wild proud blood in the widely variegated life-stream of Glasgow.

That life-stream is indeed so variegated, and the way in which it flows and beats is so full of change, that it is impossible to name or even to describe one Glasgow type. There are too many Glasgow types, and they come from too many backgrounds to be summed up in one individual. There are, however, certain general characteristics which the city has given to its children, even to the most Whiggishly prosperous of them – warmheartedness combined with a love of combat and dispute, liveliness, a lively curiosity, and a capacity for intellectual activity combined with an odd streak of complacency, real generosity in material and spiritual things combined with a very material respect for wealth, a love of sentiment that it would be unfair to call sentimentality, combined with a sharp practicality, a love of, or at least a respect for, beauty in art, combined with a native coarseness in custom and expression, a warm, deep, and indeed infectious love for their city that sometimes expresses itself in a prickly and uncertain defensiveness about it and finally a patriotic love for Scotland and Scottish things, a distrust of English manners and ways and politics combined with an increasingly wistful pride in the title of the 'Second City of the Empire'. It is this last combination that is responsible for the fact that Glasgow is the centre of the liveliest forms of Scottish Nationalism and the seat of the most obdurate opposition to it.

If it is difficult to think of one representative Glasgow type it is impossible to choose one for Edinburgh. This is not because the Edinburgh character is not definite and recognizable – it is one of the most definite of city characters in Europe – but because the Capital of Scotland is above everything else a city of individuals; yet each individual is radically and obviously of Edinburgh. 'You can often recognize a face as an Edinburgh face when you are far from Scotland, but you will never confuse one Edinburgh face with another, either in or away from the city. They are never the same.'

The character of the people of Edinburgh is obviously the product not only of the past but of the physical fact of their city. Stevenson in his long and excellent essay on Edinburgh smiled at his fellow citizens for their prosaic behaviour and demeanour going about their daily business, in the daily drab clothes of Victorianism against so extravagantly theatrical a background. One sees what he meant, but one is bound to defend one's own grandfathers, Stevenson's contemporaries, and indeed the inhabitants of Edinburgh at any time since the building of modern Edinburgh a hundred and fifty years ago by pointing out that it would be impossible to dress and behave in a manner suitable to the tremendous stage of this city. Nonetheless, that stage and the way it has been set up over the centuries has profoundly influenced the character of those who live and act upon it to-day.

It is easy for the visitor, if he comes first in favourable weather, to be at once impressed by the sensationally dramatic appearance of Edinburgh. He will as soon as he rrives see the Castle on its rock, and he will think of it as dominating the whole place in a more forceful way than any castle dominates any city in Europe, for it lies at the heart of Edinburgh and is visible from every quarter. Then, as he moves about, he will become aware of other elements in the Edinburgh scene, and will look upon the Castle for what it is, only one, if physically the most obvious, of the many large and dramatic things about the Capital of Scotland: it is no more than the culminating point of the 'Old Town', the medieval city that hangs high above the late-eighteenth-century and modern town. And in that 'New Town' itself there are gardens, wide streets, gracious squares, crescents, octagons, and 'places' designed nobly and with an aristocratic sense of space as well as of design. All this he will soon discover.

But it will not take the visitor long to perceive also that this contrast of jumbled medievalism high upon the central rock with the architecture of the Augustan age spread at its feet, this romantic steepness and this ordered spaciousness around it is contained within the bounds of a quite comprehensible town, a small and homogeneous capital whose bundaries on many sides are marked and held by large and unalterable facts of nature. While still standing at the centre of Edinburgh and not necessarily on one of our many high places he can see the huge mass of Arthur's Seat that at the east end of the city and nearly within the suburbs looms immediately above the Palace of Holyroodhouse. Looking south and again at our very gates there are the Pentlands, our guardian range whose highest peaks are two thousand feet. And if he turns to the north he will see the New Town descending steeply, abruptly, but still graciously to the shores of the Firth of Forth. Standing at one of the intersections of George

Street he can look out across this wide arm of the sea with its 'immemorial traffic' upon it and see in the distance the shores and hills of the ancient Kingdom of Fife.

These then are the obvious and impressive things about Edinburgh which any visitor can hardly fail to notice. Nor, because of their obviousness, do they become any less impressive to or less regarded by the inhabitant of Edinburgh who loves his city. As he lives year in year out in the place he will observe many subtleties of change in these grand and dramatic circumstances, and will notice a thousand tricks and effects played and made upon them by our soft and perpetually changing northern light. He may even in his admiration for this shifting, changing, yet always massive townscape come to have an affection for Edinburgh when she is in her most scowling mood, when rain lashes the place into an all-pervading glistening grey or when the 'haar' rises from the sea and silently cloaks the steepness and the graciousness of it in a physically disagreeable mist.

These obvious yet fundamental things about the shape and structure of Edinburgh have done much to influence her history and have had their effect on the character of her people. As a capital city set upon a rock and well defended on most sides, Edinburgh has been for centuries imperturbable. This imperturbability has been strengthened by the fact that Edinburgh has grown without violent change. She has never been sacked, put to the sword, or completely burnt down. Her inhabitants have never had to flee from her. Nor in more modern times has she (like the larger industrial centres) had to endure mass immigration.

This is reflected in the character of the Edinburgh people, who have a name for imperturbability. They are

ar from being unemotional, but do not express emotion
easily, preferring to cover it under formality or an oddly
formal eccentricity. This fact is often noticed, and with
irritation, by Glasgow folk. Nor can it be denied that Edinburgh people often do give the impression of complacency, a complacency which angered Robert Louis
Stevenson in his rebellious days and before he fell in love
with his maternal city all over again and from the other
side of the world.

Edinburgh's long history, combined with the fact that
the eighteenth century was her most famous period and
the period which has left its physical impress most obviously upon her, has bred in her people a strong formality
in manner. There is no city in the United Kingdom
where the eighteenth century lingers more strongly in
habit and behaviour. This formality in porters, hotel servants, shopkeepers as well as in lawyers, ministers, and
professional men often surprises visitors from England. It
does not (if one may correct a Glasgow impression once
more) spring from snobbishness or from lack of kind
hearts. It is just a habit – and one which many of us do
not find disagreeable.

Despite this formality the Capital of Scotland is filled
with strongly individual individuals, and has a larger proportion of native eccentrics than has any other town in
Britain. Yet even these eccentrics, if they are of the true
Edinburgh breed, conduct their eccentricities with an
odd formality, in a kind of pattern of peculiarity suitable
to the extravagant pattern in the appearance and background of the town. It would be too much to say that that
background was itself responsible for their eccentricities,
but perhaps in common with Edinburgh's long individual
history and with the still lingering eighteenth-century

tradition it has helped to make them possible.

Imperturbability tinged with complacency, formalit
in expression and habit, a strong sense of individualit
that runs easily to eccentricity – you can find all thes
qualities in all classes in Edinburgh, amongst the poor a
well as the prosperous, in the public houses, small shop
and wynds and closes of the High Street in the poores
part of the Old Town as well as in the clubs, lawyers
offices, and what remains of the drawingrooms of the Nev
Town. Nevertheless it is as difficult to name a 'type' fo
Edinburgh as it is for Glasgow. There are some notabl
figures in fiction that come to mind. Stevenson's Weir o
Hermiston, Stevenson's Barbara Grant and some of hi
old ladies, Scott's gossips in *The Heart of Midlothian*, hi
legal characters in *Guy Mannering*, and one or two others
Let it be admitted, however, that not even Scott was abl
to do for his own Edinburgh what he did for Glasgow ir
Bailie Nicol Jarvie. The Edinburgh patriot may however console himself by the reflexion that despite their
definiteness of character his fellow citizens are all toc
much themselves to be summed up in one 'type'. 'Amids
incomparable individuals how can one be pre-eminent?'

The strong flavour of the Edinburgh character stil
persists remarkably in our present shifting and uncertain
mid twentieth century. Like the fretted skyline of the Old
Town seen from Princes Street, like the massive Augustan
fronts of the houses in the New Town, it seems to have
survived and with but small effect of change not only wars
but the more insidious effects of cinemas, the wireless, dog
tracks, the pools, the internal combustion engine, the
licensing laws, and other eccentricities of our age. Like
that skyline and those houses it remains as a reassurance
and a balm for the traveller returning to his native city.

But the returning traveller would be guilty of sentimentality, of a mere middle-aged and comfortable nostalgia if he were to think of the Capital of Scotland only as a comforting anachronism in architecture and manners. Edinburgh, despite her long traditions and her apparent calm, is, as she has shown more than once in her history, an incalculable town. To name but one instance, there was her rise to international fame in the eighteenth century. By 1720 the effect of the Union of Parliaments on her had become so severe that she was all but abandoned. Grass grew between the cobble stones of her High Street, and men all over Scotland thought that her days as a Capital were over, that she would sink to the level of an unimportant county town. Within forty years, however, the High Street had not only driven out the encroaching grass but had become one of the most famous thoroughfares in Europe. Edinburgh's most celebrated age of genius had begun. The change had come about in an incalculable way. Edinburgh's subsequent nineteenth-century decline into complacent near provinciality was not so startling a change, but it was as strong in its effect on the reputation of the Capital. With the rise of Glasgow in the West and the increasing power of London in the South it seemed to many that Edinburgh's position as a Capital had now at last and inevitably declined beyond redemption.

To those who can remember that period of complacent provinciality Edinburgh's present vitality in Scotland is yet another and happy instance of her incalculability. For now, half way through the twentieth century, she is vital once more. It is not only the success of her annual international Festival (one of the boldest and most remarkable civic ventures in Britain since the war) nor the reign of three consecutive outstanding Lord Provosts, nor yet the imaginative plans which Edinburgh is making for her future growth and internal rehabilitation, that are the main manifestations of this reawakening vitality. It is also a new or perhaps rather revived spirit in the Capital which has now begun to think of herself as a Capital, and not only in name.

For the first time since the sunset glories of the Walter Scott romantic period Edinburgh is actively aware of herself as something more than a museum of Scottish antiquities, a pleasant gentlemanly backwater in a northern province preserving within its ancient walls the customs, habits, and few remaining privileges mostly connected with the Law and the Church from the time when that province was a country. This is shown by the fact that it is in nearly every instance Edinburgh, and official Edinburgh at that, that leads Scotland in fighting the bureaucratic and centralizing influences of Westminster and London. Whatever opinion one may hold on the Nationalist question, one cannot deny that it is a sign of increasing vitality in the one-time complacent and (within Scotland) self-sufficient Edinburgh that her administration should be leading all Scotland in the preservation of civic and Scottish independence. Glasgow may be the headquarters of the most active bodies expressing and organizing the Nationalist feeling, but it is the city of Edinburgh and not the city of Glasgow that is assuming the capital function in putting their ideas into practice.

This vitality is showing itself too in the literature of Edinburgh and the eagerness with which Scottish matters in the arts are discussed, given an airing, and fought over in the modern capital. Robert Louis Stevenson would not be nearly so lonely as he was in the Edinburgh of seventy years ago were he alive to-day.

There are other signs of vitality to which he who believes in the modern Edinburgh could point with enthusiasm; but all things must have an end – even this dissertation upon the two main cities of Scotland. It would indeed have been possible to have said much more about Edinburgh and Glasgow, and not to have strayed from important Scottish themes. Between them the two places hold nearly a third of the population of the country. You may regret this fact and wish to alter it, or at least to retard the tendency that has brought it about, or you may regard this large urbanization of the south of Scotland as something inevitable of which the best has to be made. You cannot deny, however, that in a purely Scottish way (that is to say while keeping their Scottish characteristics) these two towns, only forty miles apart, are of immense, of over-shadowing importance in Scotland to-day. Their combined influence on the country is probably greater than that of London upon England. Their differing histories, their differing characters, their differing contributions to Scottish life have made what we know as modern Scotland.

But in their differences these two great Scottish cities are also complementary. That word is not only important, it is operative. It was operative in a picturesque sense in the last century; it is operative in a more practical way to-day. In the future those who live in Glasgow and Edinburgh will have to regard it as essentially operative if the Scotland which they have done so much to make is to survive as a unit in Europe.

CHAPTER FIVE

THE COUNTRY AND THE COUNTRYSIDE

'I LOVE every stick, stone, and piece of mud of Scotland, but I can't stand the people that crawl about on its surface.' So said an enthusiastic Scottish patriot at the end of last century. Extravagant though this bitter declaration of love may have been, there must have been other patriots who at times have felt as he did – particularly Scottish patriots. There are times when every lover of his country cannot but believe that the majority of his fellow countrymen are utterly opposed to his conception of his and their nation, are themselves utterly different from his own enthusiastic view of them or what he supposes to be his view of them. At such moments of near despair he may well turn for relief to the actual physical fact of the land which gave him and his compatriots birth. He will turn to the land as a child to its mother, seeking in her maternal fidelity and changelessness a solace for his fellow children's and his own inconstancy. She will always be there for him. This is for Scotsmen a particularly strong temptation – or perhaps it would be fairer to say natural desire. The land of Scotland is for Scots a ready assuagement for the disillusioned, a perpetual incitement to the indifferent and a constant joy to the happy and contented.

The intense feeling for the actual physical land of Scotland which forms so large an emotion in the Scottish character is no new thing. It has little and at its best and strongest nothing to do with the nineteenth-century romantic taste for the wild, the noble, the picturesque which in the eyes of Victorian England and of much of Europe suddenly made the little and remote country of Scotland poetically and pictorially fashionable a little more than a hundred years ago. Part of it springs naturally from the love that any patriot feels for his land, whether it be beautiful or not, merely because it is his land. This is the kind of love that made Chopin carry with him during his long exile a piece of Polish earth in a silver box. It was a lump of dried mud from one of those long undulating Galician plains that to the eye even of the most determinedly picturesquely minded have little save a kind of mournful attraction; but it was a piece of earth from his Poland – torn, partitioned, persecuted, distracted, with even its grey historic boundaries uncertain, but still his Poland. This also is the kind of love that made Robert Burns lie upon his face to kiss the soil of Scotland when he returned from one of his rare visits across the Border into England, and at one of the dullest places in the whole Scottish landscape, Gretna.

Indeed Burns' love for the land of Scotland was almost entirely of this kind. He loved the land of Scotland because it was the land which belonged to the people of Scotland, which they had fought for and held, which was peculiarly theirs, the land which has been soaked in their blood, watered with their tears, and made fruitful by their labours. He was profoundly moved by the history of the land of Scotland and was touched in the tenderest places of his mind by the domestic life of its present, its fields, its humble cottages, its old buildings, its historic rivers, but he seems to have been strangely unmoved by its beauty. For the most part of his life Burns worked upon the land in Ayrshire, and within constant, almost daily sight of one of the most lovely and variable views in all Scotland, the Arran mountains as seen from the mainland. Literally thousands of times he must have seen that which to-day can move the most obdurate of us to awe, 'the light that never was on sea or land', of the sun setting behind those mountains and into the Atlantic, yet never once in his poetry, his letters, or his recorded speech does he mention this unparalleled prospect that was his own, from his own part of his own Scotland.

Apart from this patriotic love for the land of Scotland there is in Scotsmen an hereditary affection for the fact of their country which is influenced by the simple facts of geography. Scotland for all her innumerable variations of scene and shape and weather is, all over her surface, so obviously Scotland and no other part of the earth. On three sides she is bounded by the sea and surrounded by her own hundreds of islands, and on the fourth side her short line of difference from England may not be as exact as a sea coast but is in Scottish and in many English eyes obvious and well marked. Her physical characteristics are therefore not only strong and recognizable but bounded, defined, and contained.

These physical characteristics that proclaim her for herself and mark the difference between her and her Southern and contiguous neighbour can be described in terms of science, of geology, and climate. They can also be recognized even if they cannot be defined by any Scotish child who, knowing his own country, travels into England for the first time in his adolescence. He will observe differences in manner, custom, speech, and building, and all these will strike him as strange; but, being a child, and closer to nature than his elders, it will be the difference in the quality of the country that will catch his attention.

Later on, when he is older, and if he has the curiosity to find out, he may learn the reason for these differences between the land of England and the land of Scotland, and may know in more exact terms the physical characteristics of his own country. He may discover that as the geologists have long made clear, and as Mr Ian Finlay so succinctly puts it, 'Scotland had begun her fight against unceasing and peculiarly ferocious invasion long before man made his appearance.' He will learn that Scotland has been the target of conflicting forces from West and East, that her naturally hard rock mass thrust out thus into the North Atlantic has had to face and resist (not always successfully) not only the fury of the Northern ocean gales but the long ceaseless wash of the great ocean rollers. One glance at the map of the romantically fretted west coast of Scotland will illustrate this for him more vividly than any scientific account. What he will not, however, so easily perceive is that on the apparently more placid eastern coast the extremes of temperature have combined with the wash of tide and the greater malleability of the land to threaten the structure of Scotland as dangerously if more insidiously. He may learn also that his country's resistance to this immemorial assault of sea and wind and water and ice has rested upon the natural hardness of her material upon the west and the fact that Nature has built for her, save in her central and protected plain, rampart upon rampart of great hills. And it is at the English border that these hills end.

Later on he may learn all these and many other things, but as a child, though he may feel the difference between the land of England and his own land in a hundred ways, he will probably content himself at first by merely saying in mild surprise, 'How flat England is!' Later again, if he stays in or frequently visits England, he may learn to love the soft contour of the English uplands, the wide rich meadows, the moorlands of the South West and the whole garden-like prospect of his southern neighbour's land. But it is unlikely that he will ever be deeply impressed by the mountains of the Lake District. Later still, no matter how much he may be lulled and delighted by the comfortable beauty of the English scene, he will find his thoughts and his heart returning to the sometimes more barren and yet somehow more prodigal, more generous, less self-contained beauty that surrounded him in his own childhood and surrounded the childhood and the lives of those of his own race that went before him. He will grow hungry for the sight of one of his own uncultivated hillsides; and as he lets his imagination wander homewards and northwards he will not care whether it lead him to a hillside that is bare with the grey austerity of winter or garish with the colours of a northern autumn so long as it be one of the hills of his own country.

The sharp quality of this difference between the country of Scotland and the country of England (perceivable at any point at which you may cross the Border) makes an obvious appeal to the Scotsman who is conscious of his nationality. Something in his blood, which is the blood of a people who have for centuries had to fight for their existence, responds to and feels at home in a countryside so eloquent of an antique struggle against national forces. The very shape of the hills that have resisted immemorial storms, even the austerity of the more desolate moorlands that have remained unaltered for centuries, speak to him of something within himself and of a quality with which he has a profound sympathy.

But there is something more intimate, more domestic in this highly characteristic landscape which (seen either in recollection, imagination, or in fact) fills him with a sense of personal and pardonable pride. This is his own country and there is no mistake about it. Every mountain, every hill, every moorland, every sour and rancid piece of half-industrialized Lowland, every noble Western coloured prospect, every island about her coasts, every piece of indigenous building, sometimes it seems every stick and stone and piece of earth, is in his eyes obviously and unmistakably Scottish. The nation of Scotland has been made by history and geography. In the last two hundred years Scotsmen may have surrendered something of the birthright given to them by history, and by the men who went before them, but they cannot so easily lose what has been left to them by Nature and geography. The land of Scotland remains inviolate.

Other European countries whose patriots may have this same intense feeling for their land do not always have this geographical support and consolation. However much Chopin may in exile have yearned for the brown earth of his forbidden Poland, neither he nor any other Pole could have told you where that brown earth was in essence different from the earth of the great plains of Europe and Russia that surrounded it. Save for the man-made fact of the Polish language and Polish customs of those who so passionately possessed and cultivated this part of the world's surface, there was nothing to mark the places where Poland ended and where the ambience of the great Central European plains began. This is not so in Scotland; and the traditional and intense devotion of the

Scot to the land of Scotland comes in part from his unspoken, often undefined and half-conscious recognition of this fact.

This was the emotion that so profoundly, perhaps most profoundly of all, animated Walter Scott; for there was in all that rich character nothing so deep and integral as his love for his country. And it was this emotion that illuminated his dying moments when, after the long painful journey from Rome through Venice, Munich, Heidelberg, Rotterdam, and London he lay by his open windows at Abbotsford, heard the sound of Tweed and watched his hills of home fade into their last and endless night. Others of his compatriots, countless others, have felt what Scott felt about the land of Scotland, many maybe with equal intensity, but none have expressed it, or perhaps rather made it felt to others with such force as did Scott. He made it felt not only in his written work but in his life and in the strong impress of his personality upon his countrymen, an impress which is still most powerfully felt in Scotland to-day. For some of us Scott was not only the richest character, but the most nearly complete and certainly the most lovable of men that our country has produced. Burns may have sprung like a tongue of flame from the glowing embers of the Scotland that he knew, but Scott is himself so much all Scotland that he is like a deep-banked fire of patriotism. Merely to think of him, merely to see in imagination that noble ruddy Scots face with its crown of white hair, even to write his name is to feel something of the glow of his feeling for his country, which has not yet lost its warmth, though the fire which made it was extinguished nearly a hundred and twenty years ago.

Scott's writings, particularly his poetry, may have been

responsible for much of the susceptibility which made Scotland fashionably beautiful, or at least romantically picturesque, in the nineteenth century, but there was little if any of this nonsense about Scott's own attitude towards the land of Scotland. He was of course the child of, as well as one of the creators of, his own age, and he could not but have been affected by what poor Mr Ogilvie in Dr Johnson's presence in a memorable scene half a century earlier called Scotland's 'noble prospects'. Mountain scenery, the wilder Highland landscapes, the impetuous rush of a Northern river in spate, the gloom and grandeur of a remote hill-surrounded loch, all these and their like could move him to admiration and pleasure as indeed they can move any man of sensibility to-day. But the fact that he could occasionally write jingling verse about them as well as noble descriptions did not mean that this kind of romantic admiration was the basis of his love of Scotland. Indeed it hardly affected it at all, and was no more than a decoration, a pleasant accessory to it.

Scott was a man of the world as well as of Scotland. As a boy and as a young man he had been well and thoroughly educated according to the best traditions of his time. His insatiable thirst for knowledge, his facility in language and his love of wide reading carried and continued his education throughout his life; and his remarkable memory enabled him to garner the fruits of it to the end. He was above all a man of generous and wide appreciation. His love of the land of Scotland then, though it sprang from the same simple and deep emotion that he shared with Burns and many others less vocal and utterly unknown Scotsmen, was a much larger (though no less intense) affair in the way in which it expressed and exercised itself. He knew so much and relished so much. There was no corner of the remotest part of his country which did not speak to his immensely well-stocked mind of some part of her history. The whole land, in a thousand different voices in different places and at different times, was eloquent to him of her past. Combined with his natural love for the small, highly individual country that had given him birth was the pertinacious curiosity of the antiquarian, the convictions and the sentiment of the historian, and the passion of the poet.

And it was in this last, his poetic attitude, that he most clearly and forcibly expressed his feelings. It was the poet in him as well as the dying patriot that filled his imagination with thoughts of the beauty of the Border countryside all through that long last journey home from the Eternal City to his own eternal hills. It was the hunger for beauty, his own familiar kind of beauty, that filled him in those last weeks. Walter Scott, despite the meretriciousness of some (only some) of his verse, despite the lamentable wave of popular sentimentality that followed upon his true romanticism, was amongst the first Scotsmen to appreciate the beauty of the land of Scotland.

The beauty of Scotland is, like most aesthetic matters, not a subject open to much argument. Either you are sensible of it or you are not. In the eighteenth century, that period of intense artistic sensibility, men were almost entirely blind to the beauty of the Northern kingdom. English travellers found the austerity of the Lowlands distasteful and the wilderness of the Highlands alarming, uncomfortable and repellent, or, to use their own favourite word in its stricter and stronger contemporary meaning, 'horrid'. Scotland was in Charles Churchill's words 'a land where half-starved spiders fed upon half-starved flies'; and to visiting Englishmen the Scottish landscape seemed to confirm this. Dr Johnson, whose quick and human sympathy for the Hebrideans and their way of life testified not only to his warm heart but to the fact that in this respect he was not as other Englishmen, was unimpressed by the grandeur of Skye. And when Boswell drew his attention to the largest mountain they had seen upon their Scottish travels, he said, 'No, Sir; it is only a vast protuberance.' Even Scotsmen themselves, if they came from the Lowlands, were insensible of beauty north of the Highland line, and disregarded those parts of the Western seaboard (lying, as it were, at their own back doors) which now seem to us to be amongst the loveliest scenery in Europe.

The popularity of the romantic movement in the early part of the nineteenth century changed all this. If in early references it may appear that the present writer has been too scornful of the results of this movement as it affected Scotland, let him make amends by admitting this. Despite all its exaggerations, with all its occasional falsity and sentimentality, if it had not been for this movement we would still be blind to the beauty of over more than half our country. After the clearances and enforced emigrations, which, for political reasons, would have occurred in any event, the Highlands might well have developed into a rich sportsman's paradise; but there would have been even amongst these visitors no appreciation of the land over which they shot and the waters in which they fished. And to do them justice most nineteenth-century sportsmen, as we can see from their memoirs, did have some feeling of this kind. But what is of far greater importance, it is unlikely that the eyes of the ordinary people of Scotland would have been opened to what now seems to them to be an inheritance of incalculable value – the beauty of their own land. The cities and towns of Scotland are to-day full of young men and women, and middle-aged people too, who at weekends, at holiday time and, indeed, as often as they can go out into the sometimes bare, sometimes prodigal beauty of the Scottish countryside and find there not only physical but spiritual recuperation – though they would never dream of speaking of it in these terms.

Few of these native lovers of the Scottish Highlands and the Scottish country have heard more than a line or two of the more hackneyed quotations from Scott's verse, or have read any of his Scottish novels. Fewer still are aware of the minor artistic productions in verse, romance, and painting on 'romantic Scotland' that followed upon Scott's tremendous initial impetus. Nor would they think much of them if they could read or see them. They would probably consider them silly and meretricious. And this would be not only because most of them are artistically uneducated or incurious but because they are of a generation that has grown up to appreciate the beauty of their country naturally and therefore genuinely. They do not need the stimulus of romantic or sentimental art to arouse in them a hunger which they were born with, the hunger for the beauty of wide moorland spaces, of mountains rich in the colours of the Western seaboard or grey and mysterious, of summer lochans dreaming unruffled in the high clefts of hills, peat-stained burns tumbling from one amber-coloured pool to another until they reach the river in the green glen. Genuine and unselfconscious though this now popular feeling for the beauty of the land of Scotland may be, the ordinary people of Scotland would not have possessed it and enjoyed it as they do if it had not been for the now long spent and exhausted romantic movement of the last century.

Despite the fact that there are certain recognizable characteristics in all the Scottish countryside which give it its individual quality, and which so sharply differentiate it from England, that quality is highly varied. This variation discovers itself both in appearance and in climate at many different times and in many different places which are often quite near to each other. In general, however, the main line of difference runs from North to South; and the difference is between East and West. It has already been emphasized in these pages that the Highland line, both ethnically and geographically, runs north-east to south-west. But the line of difference in climate, and often in the structure of the land itself, runs from the centre of the northern coast between Caithness and Sutherland down to the middle of the southern edge of Scotland in Dumfriesshire, that is where the long arm of the Solway Firth touches the borderland with England. This east-west difference is, of course, influenced by the fact that the Highland geographical line runs north-east to south-west, and it would be true to say that the most characteristic Highland scenery is in the West. But anyone who knows and feels his countryside of Scotland will recognize the often precipitous Highlands of Aberdeenshire as being essentially of Eastern Scotland, just as he will know the flats of Kintyre, of parts of Ayrshire and of Galloway to be obviously Western.

Apart from the, on the whole, more consistently grand and romantic appearance of the West, the main difference between the two halves of Scotland is in the climate; the influence of which both on the people and on the land on which they work is profound. The Western climate is soft, and the Eastern is hard with transitory periods of a lovely north-east tenderness, which touches the austerer landscape with an unexpected and rare loveliness – in itself austere. The west of Scotland is moist; and the reputation which the country as a whole has gained for raininess comes from the fact that so many visitors concentrate for business upon Glasgow and upon the Western Highlands for holidays. At the same time the other reputation which Scotland has acquired for rich and lovely colouring in her country districts also springs from the moistness of the West, to which so many tourists go. The soft Atlantic rain that can sometimes continue in spring and summer (but never in the autumn) for two or three weeks on end may have a depressing effect on all but anglers, but when it lifts it discovers an incredibly rich softness of colouring in the mountains for which it has been directly responsible. This softness of atmosphere and of colouring in the West is not however reflected in the actual physical quality of the Western land, which is hard and rocky, having withstood countless millenniums of Atlantic winter storms. On the other hand the harder-looking, climatically colder Eastern half of the country is less firm, and within the memory of man, let alone within the scope of recorded history, has changed its shape far more noticeably than has the rockier West.

Within these two halves of Scotland there are many variations. In the Eastern side the Border Hills that rise to mark the landward end of Scotland in the South are full of a mysterious allure of their own, unlike anything else in the country. They are very much not the Celtic Highlands, and yet there is about them something of the same sense of immemorial history. These descend northwards and eastwards to the wide agricultural land of the

Lothians. Across the Firth of Forth the ancient shire or, as it was once called, Kingdom of Fife marks the beginning of the North-East Lowlands which reaches its climax of climatically exposed austerity in Buchan. Round the corner and within the jaws of the Moray Firth the land becomes for the East of Scotland almost lush, and the weather mild. Northwards again the Eastern mainland ends in the barren and at times alarming beauty of Caithness. In all this near three hundred miles' length of countryside, and with all its variation of scene, the atmosphere and appearance remain indubitably Eastern and indubitably Scottish.

Similarly in the West the variation between Sutherland and the Mull of Galloway in the South is highly marked. Galloway is the strange exotic garden land of Scotland lying under the shadows of great hills and high moorlands that not only surround and protect the softer lowlands of this district but thrust themselves in and between them. Galloway is, from the visitors' point of view, one of the least known parts of Scotland. Tucked away in the south-west corner, and farther South than much of north-east England, it lies off the main route north and into Scotland. Its climate is the mildest in all the country; and indeed some who are not native to it find it oppressive. Palm trees grow there, and so do flowers that elsewhere in the United Kingdom are to be found only in the South and West of England. Yet with all this mildness, this protected and in its lower places almost hothouse air, it is as unmistakably of Scotland as is Devon of England. The high and heather-covered hills that are never out of sight, something in the quality of sea that washes its coast, proclaim it to be in the northern kingdom. Northward, the Lowlands and the green hills of Ayrshire offer an immediate contrast. Then there is the romantically fretted coast of Argyll, where the true West Highland scenery begins. It reaches its climax in the west of Inverness-shire where in the fine weather of autumn the colour as well as the form of the mountains are to the visitor sometimes almost overpowering. This luxuriance changes in Sutherland to grey grandeur and to mournful desolation, culminating in the extreme north-west tip in the finely-named Cape Wrath, between which and the American continent there is nothing but a waste of seas.

This East and West division of the land of Scotland is clearly marked, and is strongly felt as well as recognized by all who live in her. There is, however, one central part of the country that lies clean aross the main division and preserves its strong yet important individuality. Scenically it is not striking, and can be dull and unattractive: most visitors pass through it without paying much attention to it, not realizing that in a sense it is the heart of Scotland. This is the central plain (though it would not look like a plain to an English child visiting Scotland for the first time) that lies between the Highlands and the Border Hills. It is the cradle of the Scottish nation, and nearly all the important events in our history have happened in it. Both Edinburgh and Glasgow lie upon its south-eastern and western beginnings. Perth is its most important northern point, and the historic but now sleepy town of Stirling was its fortified point. Geographically it is, apart from Caithness, the most lowland part of Scotland, and despite continual Celtic influence from the Northern rampart of hills its population is predominantly Lowland, with all the strains that go to make the Lowland character fairly equally mixed in it. In its rather featureless appearance it is the least obviously Scottish part of

Scotland, but historically, agriculturally, and nowadays industrially it has been and is of the greatest importance to the country. On the East it is washed by the sea from whence in past centuries the Scandinavian invasions, which have so much influenced Scotland, came. But on all other sides it is surrounded by the kind of land that began where England ended in her Northern marches.

The Highlands, the Lowlands, the Border country, with all their innumerable internal differences, make up a small but highly variegated countryside which can easily be reached from the centres of all the larger Scottish towns, Edinburgh, Glasgow, Aberdeen, and Dundee. This is a fact which all classes of Scots people take advantage of, whether they live in the centre of the larger industrial districts or in the country towns. This is particularly true of to-day and of the last thirty years. Apart from his native feeling for the land which has been dealt with at some length in this chapter, the average Scot has always extracted as much pleasure in the way of sports and country pursuits from his countryside as he was able. To some foreigners in the past who surveyed with understandable distaste what seemed to them the barren austerity of the Northern country, this passion of the Scot for doing his best to enjoy his land has sometimes seemed ridiculous. Unaware, however, of the more luxuriant pleasures of Southern lands, the Scot has since the founding of his nation always been ingenious and assiduous in extracting pleasure from what would now be called 'out of doors'.

Of recent years, that is since the end of the first World War, there has been a large increase in the facilities for enjoying these out-of-door pleasures. As a result of a number of causes, some economic, some social, some coming

directly from the invention of the motor car and the bi-
cycle, the land of Scotland has been as never before thrown
open to the people of Scotland. This opening up of the
land to the people of the towns is not of course confined
to Scotland. It has been one of the happiest social tendencies all over Britain and Europe in the last gloomy
thirty years. But it is doubtful if there is any country in
Europe where this release has brought purer pleasure or
greater gusto than Scotland. It is not only that the poorer
people were in the last century more painfully constricted
in more odious industrial circumstances in Scotland than
elsewhere (though that in general is probably true), it is
also that those who had for three or four generations been
thus confined had deep in their blood a longing for their
own countryside pleasures which even a century and a
half of unnatural town-dwelling could not eradicate.

The industrial areas and towns of Scotland are, for the
most part, tightly packed and self-contained. The countryside, and often wild countryside at that, comes right up
to their edges and does not fade into them. The average
Scots townsman then does not usually have far to go
to escape. When he does escape to enjoy himself in his
own land his pleasures are these. There is probably first
of all his delight in wandering, wandering as far and as
remotely as he can within the highly variegated scenery
of his country. This may take the form of walking (the
word hiking is now fortunately dropping out of use),
bicycling, motoring, or begging lifts from lorries or indeed
any way of getting about which modern means can offer.
There are those who are inclined to deplore the effects of
this outlet of the towns upon the country of Scotland.
Apart from the unthinking selfishness of such an attitude
of mind, those who take this point of view ignore an

essential fact about the present structure of the Scottish countryside. It is far too wild and in the North and West too mountainous and too sparsely populated to be spoiled by the incursions of those young people from the towns who have the energy and enthusiasm to explore it. Rather their hearts should rejoice, upon our long summer days, to see the countless little encampments by the lochside at the head of the glen and on the moorlands, which are quite wide enough to accommodate these and many others. Now that the preservation of the lonely lovely deserts of the North solely for the use of rich sportsmen is declining, if almost at an end, they remain quite lonely and lovely enough to be able to hold double the number of Youth Hostels, lodging houses, and certified camping places without losing anything of their beauty or quality.

Then there is golf. The English reader may smile at the idea of putting forward this game as a popular sport. Let him be assured, however, that the game with us, despite mounting costs, despite the overpowering effect of its world-wide vogue in the last half century, remains an indigenous sport that is enjoyed by all classes as well as by the rich. This is partly due to the fact that for centuries golf, or a pastime roughly equivalent to golf, has been in the blood of the Scots male; it also is due to the unrivalled natural quality of the links (rather than golf courses) on which golf can be played in Scotland. In most other places in the world ingenious golf architects usually have to cut and hack at the scenery, dig for bunkers, and water the turf or encourage it by other means before a golf course can come into existence. This is not so in Scotland, which (with perhaps a remote acknowledgement to Holland of six centuries ago) is the birthplace of this infuriating but to its addicts inescapably alluring game. Golf grew up as naturally on the sandy springy turf of the East of Scotland links as did cricket in the meadows of England, and is with us quite as democratic a sport. Better, more efficient, golf may for a long time now have been played by Americans, Australians, South Africans, and, we must frankly admit it, Englishmen, but nowhere in the world does the young male take more naturally or more sweetly to it than in Scotland. There are some who regret that when he grows up he never nowadays seems to attain the proficiency of the foreign player. There are others of us who prefer to see him, as his fathers did before him, merely enjoying the game which is his heritage.

Golf, originally imported from the Low Countries, was played in Scotland before the Reformation and has continued to be one of our national sports ever since. Men were playing at something that was remotely akin to the modern game before James IV took the flower of his country to its chivalrous end at Flodden. Cardinal Beaton, who was our last historically great Catholic ecclesiastic and who was assassinated during the interregnum before Mary Stuart's reign, played it upon the links of his own St Andrews. James VII of Scotland and II of England drove his wooden ball upon the Leith links during his residence at Holyrood over a hundred years later. During the eighteenth century the game was popular amongst the Judges, Advocates, and gentry of Edinburgh, and was played by the lairds of Fife and Aberdeenshire. There is an admirable description of the contemporary golfing type to be found in Smollett's *Humphrey Clinker*. And even the Burghers of Glasgow in their less naturally suitable Western country had taken it up. But it was not until the nineteenth century that the rules and regulations of our national game hardened into anything like their present form and that it became in the eyes of the world associated with Scotland.

In the nineteenth century the strength of the cult of golf in Scotland succeeded in disseminating it all over the country and amongst all classes. It became no longer only an aristocratic, gentlemanly, and East Coast game but a national pastime, and remained almost strictly national until near the end of the century, when the rest of the world discovered it. It was in the nineteenth century that golf really began to be the truly popular Scottish sport that our fathers knew and which, despite difficulties, it still remains. It was in the 1850's, '60's, and '70's that there arose in Scotland those famous players who, coming from the humbler classes, were so great an ornament to the game, both in the style of their play and in their unforgettable personalities. It was in the latter half of the last century that the Morris family rose to that eminence from which not even the record-breaking feats of their posterity have been able to dislodge them. Tom Morris the elder and Tom Morris the younger could be easily outplayed by the science, the knowledge, the painful application, let alone the instruments of most modern golfers. But in any golfing society worthy of the name it is sufficient to mention some authentic story or saying that derives from these two working-class Scottish golfers born in an East Coast fishing town for a reverent hush to fall upon the assembly.

The Morrises were outstanding, and as long as the game lasts will be immortal representatives of this type of Scottish golfer who began in boyhood as caddies and who worked their way up and into the game until they became integral parts of its tradition. There were, however, hundreds of others, some of them anonymous, others whose names still linger. They were sons of the soil, for the most part their own sandy East Coast soil that is washed and influenced by the grey North Sea. Golf was for some of them their livelihood, for others it was their life; but whoever they were they took it as easily and as leisurely as they lived in those quieter days in which most golfers of their kind knew every blade of grass upon the short turf of their native links but seldom played upon a course more than ten miles from home. With their long unsmiling East Coast faces, their long silences broken only by dry comments (some of which have passed into the lore of the game) they seemed to some Southern visitors to treat golf with a terrifying seriousness. They did not: they treated it with no more seriousness than they did eating, drinking, begetting children, tilling the soil, or gathering the harvest of fish from the sea by their own coasts. They lived it, but they did not live for it. At any rate they expended upon it far less nervous concentration, far less painful devotion, and far less technical seriousness than do the modern high priests of the game (whether professional or amateur) with their three or four sets of clubs with fifteen different clubs in each set, their portmanteaux of enormous bags, their gadgets, their white plus fours, white caps, and white golfing shoes, their chilling self-discipline, their neurotic inability to make a putt without five minutes of self-torturing deliberation, their endless jargonated 'shop', their itinerant and attendant masseurs.

From the tradition founded by these men, carried on by their sons, their brothers, and their relatives, and not least by those whom they taught the art of enjoying as well as playing golf springs the true democratic attitude towards the game which even now survives in Scotland. They were the forerunners of still living and still traditional caddies and professionals of St Andrews and other famous Scottish golfing centres; but they were something more. If it had not been for them the school-boys, the impecunious students, the young city clerks, the elderly failures, and many others whom no one outside Scotland would associate with this game (now thought of elsewhere as plutocratic) would not at weekends still be streaming out of the towns to play on the links on which their grandfathers played before them – and often paying no higher a fee. Perhaps if it had not been for these old forerunners St Andrews City would not have kept one of her civic glories till as late as 1948 – that of allowing all her ratepayers to play free upon the most famous links in the world.

If ever a game grew naturally out of a particular soil, golf grew out of the substance of the Scottish land. If ever a game was in its origins shaped by a national character, it was golf as played by Scotsmen. If ever the history and growth of a game can be used to illustrate the character of the nation that invented it, golf can illustrate certain elements in the Scottish mind and behaviour. The fact that, though golf after a fashion has become as world-wide and as prevalent as influenza, it remains with difficulty but persistently traditional in Scotland is a point worthy of note in the Scottish character.

There is a strong temptation for the present writer to devote an even longer and far more enthusiastic divaga-tion to the other great and democratic pleasure which the Scotsman extracts from his land, or more strictly his waters – trout fishing. The temptation is strong, because not only is this one of the few native delights, possibly the only one, which for him does not decline but grows with years, it is also a subject on which he can listen and talk endlessly, read voluminously, and when permitted write lengthily. Trout fishing in Scotland has been written about in countless books. There is always room for another one. But it is a subject on which the true devotee is not prepared to compromise. Either one lets oneself go over pages or confines oneself to the barest statement of the position. In these circumstances a paragraph will have to serve the purpose.

The surest way of getting into conversation in even the most uncommunicative part of the Lowlands is to walk down the main street of a town, entering shops, taverns, and public places where you can, carrying a trout rod and landing net. If golf is in Scotland more democratic than elsewhere, trout fishing is completely so: it ignores all distinctions of class and wealth. This is one of the delightful characteristics of anglers all over the world – and is especially true in England amongst that excellent band of brethren somewhat unjustly called 'coarse fishers'. It is, through no fault of the English however, not true of trout fishing there – at least in the South where the trout perforce remains for the most part the rich man's prey. In Scotland the brown trout is the most plentiful and the hardiest of native fish. The large number of species of coarse fish which give such a delightful variety to fishing in England either do not exist with us or, with the exception of the pike, are rare. We make up for this, however, by the immense number of our brown trout. This number may have been reduced by the increase of town-living anglers in the last hundred years, by the facility which modern transport gives them to reach once remote rivers and lochs, and most severely of all by modern and mechanical wholesale poaching methods. But despite all the

THE COUNTRY AND THE COUNTRYSIDE

multiplication of his enemies the Scottish trout survives and, in places, himself multiplies. His average size is smaller than that of the South of England trout that inhabits the chalk streams, but he can grow larger than any trout across the Border. The biggest Scottish trout yet caught was 39¾ lb. The pursuit and capture of the brown trout then has immemorially been one of the favourite sports of those who live in Scotland. It still is.

Perhaps one more paragraph may be allowed: indeed, in fairness it cannot be avoided; for there are also the brown trout's more showy but not more nobly born relatives, the sea trout and the salmon, which must be mentioned. Salmon fishing by rod, as apart from the netting at river mouths, is at its best a moneyed man's pursuit. This is partly because the best salmon waters are still preserved, and partly because it is a much more chancy sport than trout fishing. A man may well decide to take a fortnight's salmon fishing, and because of unfavourable weather return empty handed. A disaster of this kind would be incredible in a fortnight's trout fishing. And so the average not too leisured angler who has only a week or so for holiday in the year and restricted weekends prefers to bank on the comparative certainty of trout. Still, it would be a mistake to class salmon fishing in Scotland with deer stalking and similar rich men's enjoyments from the land. There are a number of salmon-fishing associations connected with the major Scottish rivers and lochs to which working men can and do belong in large numbers. But they cannot go far for their sport, and usually live near the scene of their pleasure. Few working-class anglers go out after salmon from the large towns. That beautiful and exciting fish the sea trout is, in Scotland, less rigorously preserved than the salmon, but like the

T.S. - 5   129

salmon he is more chancy than the brown trout, and yo
usually have to go further to get him. But whether it b
the lordly salmon, the noble sea trout, or gentlemanl
brown trout of equally ancient lineage, the *salmo* family t
which all three belong provide Scotsmen of all classes an
conditions with one of the main pleasures which they ge
from their countryside.

Chief amongst other traditional Scottish countrysid
sports is curling. For the benefit of the uninitiated thi
might briefly (but how inadequately) be described as a
kind of bowls played with large flat stones upon the ice
The game in Scotland is over six centuries old and ha
probably a longer though less well documented histor
than golf. It is known as 'the roaring game', not only, we
suspect, because of the agreeable deep resonance that th
stones make as they glide over the ice, but also because o
the large amount of passionate shouting in which th
players traditionally indulge. Those who look upon the
Scot as a man not much given to the expression of hi
emotions would change their opinions if they could b
present at the closing stages of the 'Bonspeil', as it i
called, at the Perthshire loch of Carsebreck when the
North of Scotland curls against the South. The grey and
white evening air is filled with shouts, wild cries, and
strange, half forgotten oaths that carry far over the ice
and in the frosty air. As twilight falls you can dimly see
respectable lawyers, doctors, ministers, as well as local
poachers, miners, and farm labourers raising their hands
above their heads in agonized imprecation or writhing
in supplication as they implore their side to 'soop it up,
soop it up' – that is, sweep the ice in front of the stone so
that it may glide on the more easily towards the centre
of the ring. There is a charming little picture by Sir

George Harvey in the National Gallery of Scotland painted about a hundred years ago. It is called 'The Curlers' and most admirably catches this spirit of Scotch abandon which the game of curling is able, as no other, to provide.

Nowadays the invention of the indoor ice rink has made the game more easy, more accessible to busy townsfolk, less dependent upon the weather and therefore less of an occasion, less of a long looked for event upon which the passions may be let loose. It is difficult in an atmosphere compounded out of the smells of chemically manufactured ice and underneath an arched dome of concrete or lath and plaster illuminated by artificial light to shout and storm and entreat and writhe and weep for joy in the old traditional Scots curling fashion. There are those too who, looking gloomily upon these new curlers who fix up their games of an evening a week ahead as regularly as they would a visit to the cinema, say that the old curling spirit in Scotland is dying. They add with an understandable *schadenfreude* the observation that Nature seems to have recognized this fact by giving us in Scotland fewer and fewer true curling winters as the years go by. The facts of our weather, however, are against them. Winter after winter, for at least one week in the year, the lochs and little suburban ponds freeze over, and the old faithfuls come out again to 'throw the stane' and shout and storm and congratulate each other in their own fearsome language as their fathers did before them – as their sons, in all probability, will continue to do after them.

Apart from these the prime and customary pleasures which the Scot enjoys in his countryside there are others, some old and some new. There is shinty, a savage kind of Celtic hockey enjoyed in the Highlands. And as a newer

Highland sport there has been some attempt to introduce
ski-ing on the longer and higher Northern slopes that are
in winter remotely accessible to road traffic. Whether
this will ever become more than an occasional and exotic-
ally supported winter pastime remains to be seen. Football in both forms of Association and Rugby can hardly
be described as a countryside pursuit except when remote
country towns meet to play each other. Despite its immense popularity, therefore, it does not come within the
scope of this chapter. It is worth pointing out, however,
that in some form or another the game is of a respectable
antiquity in Scotland. In the time of the early Stewart
kings, when the menace of English military might was
still a potent fear, laws were passed curtailing the popular sport of football so that men might be encouraged to
spend more time practising archery.

In the eyes of many foreigners shooting, in its various
forms, is looked upon as one of the first of Scottish
countryside pursuits. This is not so. Apart from a few
rough shoots, and apart from farmers who shoot over
their land, mostly for the pot, shooting and particularly
stalking in Scotland is a wealthy man's pleasure; and our
unrivalled grouse moors and deer forests (or those of them
that are still preserved) are enjoyed as much by wealthy
cosmopolitans as by wealthy or territorially wealthy
natives. As long as the Northern part of our country remains wild and desolate, and as long as it harbours the
often extremely wild life that at present inhabits it, Scotland will be an attraction for sportsmen from the South
and from overseas, as well as to the nearer kind. But
in the nature of things shooting over our moors or forests
can never become a native, let alone a popular, Scottish
countryside pleasure.

Wandering in the remoter parts of the country, mountain climbing, trout fishing, salmon fishing, golf, curling, shinty, sailing along the coasts and amidst the islands, these and other summer and winter pursuits are the main pleasures Scots people get from their countryside to-day. For the most part they are traditional and have a fairly respectable history in the literature devoted to them. It is significant, however, that the largest amount of contemporary writing, whether in the form of books or journalism, is devoted to the most modern and by far the most popular of all – the wandering in and the exploration of the remoter Scottish countryside. This, as has been said earlier in this chapter, is something that the modern Scot, and particularly the town-dweller, has within the last thirty or so years discovered for himself. Whether in mountain climbing, in walking, or through any form of transport of which he can avail himself, he is enjoying the unique quality of his country with all the gusto of a new-found delight.

Unique is a strong word, but it can be used about the as yet unsullied beauty of certain parts of Scotland. Our nation is in many things composed of extremes, sometimes complementary to each other, sometimes violently opposed. Scottish history is full of the clash of extremes; the Scottish temperament is inclined to run to extremes of thought and of behaviour; and most certainly the appearance of the countryside of Scotland presents many extremes in the most striking ways. There is not only the contrast between East and West, between Highland and Lowland, between the austerity of Buchan and the luxuriance of Galloway, between the Border Hills and the central plain which they guard, and many other contiguous contrasts, there is also the contrast of the extremes of ugliness and of beauty. There are certain parts of Scotland where the combination of a naturally depressing landscape with a man-made squalor can produce as ugly an effect as can be found anywhere. It is not necessary to name these parts, nor, fortunately, are they large; but all of us, and some visitors, know them. There are also larger tracts of land in the North-West where the natural beauty is the equal of any in Europe and where the quality of that beauty is unique. Between these extremes of what is repellent and what is infinitely alluring to the eye there are many gradations and other contrasts of scenery that are austere and scenery that is comfortable, scenery that is domestic in quality or grand in its effect. The true lover of the Scottish country will relish all these, but in the end he will have to admit that it is in the Highlands, and most of all in the Highlands of the West and North by the Atlantic seaboard, that the ultimate and unique beauty of Scotland lies.

Ultimate was the adjective that the Ancient Romans applied to Orkney and Shetland when they called them *Ultima Thule*. It is a word which seems far more applicable to the geographically not so remote Western Highlands. For here, so it appears to anyone who has been fortunate enough to enjoy them in the full glory of good weather, and who has fallen under their enchantment, is the ultimate concentration of loveliness in scenery lying ultimately upon the shores of that ocean which our forefathers for millenniums looked upon as the edge of the world.

When they are lapped in the long calm of midsummer sunshine, or in the briefer but more highly coloured beauty of an autumn day there is nothing quite like them in our continent. The present writer knows Europe well,

and is a passionate European. He assures the reader that
this is no narrow patriotism but the fruit of experience
and an ardent curiosity for natural scenery that makes
him say this. The Alps and the Pyrenees are grander and
can inspire more awe, but they lack the colour and the
softness and the mystery of these Western Scottish mountains by the Atlantic. The fiords of Norway and the great
coloured cliffs of the Faroe Islands with the Atlantic swell
murmurous two thousand feet below them are more impressive, but in some odd way that it is difficult to define
more depressing, less generous of themselves. The Tatra
Mountains that rise like a wall in the South of Poland
are a welcome sight to the traveller who has voyaged
for days across the Central European plain, but they are
not to be compared with our sea-washed Western hills.
The isles and mountain coasts of Greece are as spectacular and speak to one as eloquently of the past, but the
clarity of the Mediterranean sun while it wonderfully
illuminates them gives them a sharpness, a hardness,
which the Western Highlands are without. It deprives
them too of that marvellous self-contained luminosity
which is the chief benison of the Northern and Western
light. In the North and in the West upon a fine day it
seems that the rocks and the stones and the grass and the
heather and the mountains and the sea and the lochs do
not so much reflect the light (throw it back directly to you
as in the South) but give it out from themselves gently,
richly, luminously.

There are, of course, days, sometimes weeks, when this
softness, this luminosity of scene, which is a product of
moist atmosphere as well as of the slanting Northern light,
has to be paid for. It is then that, for long periods, all this
prodigal beauty is blotted out by mist and drifting rain.

It may be blotted out, but it cannot be forgotten by those who have enjoyed even only one day of it at its best. It is there, lying under all this grey and silver damp ambience and will re-emerge. We are content to wait for it.

What did our forefathers, our emotional, poetic Celtic forefathers who lived for over a thousand years in these scenes that appear to our modern eyes of so paradisal a beauty, think of them? Were they unaffected by them, did they have to wait like their Lowland and more Southern neighbours for the Romantic Movement to open their eyes to it all? It is difficult to believe so, sometimes almost impossible; yet how can we tell? What evidence have we? Only in snatches of Gaelic poetry here and there that has come down to us, poetry that was for the most part unrecorded and, in Dr Johnson's Augustan but melodious phrase 'floated in the breath of the people for a millennium', only in the occasional cry of nostalgia uttered by an exile two hundred years ago or in the mournful songs of the emigrants who were thrust out across the Atlantic, to eat their hearts out – on the shores of the New World, only in these fragments do we catch hints of what they thought.

In the distant past Gaelic poetry was mostly concerned with action, heroism, warfare, and occasionally love and religion. Later (but still well before the nineteenth century and before the romantic attitude towards scenery had been discovered) there are a number of references in Gaelic literature which show that the native Gael was far from insensitive to the colour and form and the appeal of his land. There is a kind of physical sensuousness in his poetic mention rather than description of the redness of the deer that troop across the hill, and of the form and colour of the hill itself, of the rowan trees, the heather and the rocks, the clarity of the water and the silver of the waterfall.

Here are some verses from a poem by an anonymous early eighteenth century poet in Kintyre, one of the quieter, more douce, and least Highland parts of the West – still very much of the West and of Gaeldom. The poem is highly characteristic of the Gaelic way of dealing with nature, a highly detached but exuberant and detailed way. And though the translation, which is literal, may not suggest lyricism, the English-speaking reader is assured that the original burns with the authentic 'hard, gem-like flame'.

Moladh Chinn-tìre

Is fochlasach biolaireach a fuarain,
    An achlais gach cluain is gach tulaich,
A' brùchdadh mar chriostal an uachdar
    'Na h-ìocshlaint fhionnair bhuadhaich mhilis.

A magha seisneil deisneil rioghail,
    An lìonmhor fear-sìolchuir 'san earrach;
'San fhoghmhar greadhnach meadhrach uallach,
    Dualach sguabach cruachach torrach.

A creaga truideach crotach calmnach,
    Murbhuach'leach sgarbhnach a calaidh,
Gèadhach lachach de gach seòrsa,
    Dobhranach rònanach ealach.

Praise of Kintyre

Rich in brook-lime and water-cresses is every
Jet of fresh water that gushes forth like crystal
in the hollow of each green pasture and knoll —
a cool sweet and satisfying cordial

In her fields, so pleasant and elegant and noble,
sowers of seed congregate in the spring; in the
autumn the fields look joyful, gay, ecstatic, rich in
the tresses of crops, in sheaves, in stacks of corn.

Her beetling cliffs are alive with starlings and doves;
into her ports and harbours flock northern divers
and cormorants as well as wild geese, wild duck
otters, seals, and swans.

Two hundred years later an English poet wrote of his
Shropshire:

> Loveliest of trees the cherry now
> Is hung with bloom along the bough,
> And stands about the woodland ride,
> Wearing white for Eastertide.

And then proceeded in the sweet arithmetic of his verse to
calculate how much of his 'three score years and ten'
were left to him to 'look at things in bloom'. There is
something in common between the Gaelic version of the
old anonymous Kintyre poem and the modern, and now
classic English lyric. But it is significant that the Gaelic
was composed two hundred years before *The Shropshire
Lad*, at a time when English, and indeed all European
poets were writing of Nature, if they wrote of her at all,
in a very different strain, and when it never occurred to
anyone to take this rapturous delight in her simplest
manifestations.

Poems like *Moladh Chinn-tìre* drift down to us by chance
from a forgotten, one had almost said a golden, age of
Gaeldom, before the great disasters had happened, before
the land had been despoiled and its people thrust out and
away. It was a period of comparative happiness when the
Scottish Gael could take a simple and immediate pleasure

in his own circumstances, and without that mournful strain which is the inevitable undertone of all his poetry since the collapse of his way of life half-way through the eighteenth century. But in that later and sadder verse and in much of the Gaelic writing of the time that would not claim to be verse one can detect again the note of physical yearning for the Highlands.

The simplest things from one's past life admittedly become precious to one in recollection when one has lost all; and it is perhaps easier to recall the details rather than the great things in a scene from which one is forever separated. The intensity, however, with which the songs of the emigrants and the letters which they wrote speak of the details of their lost homeland shows that they must have appreciated those details when they had seen them, and had known them about their everyday lives. In the words of the anonymous, often quoted, but obstinately beautiful *Canadian Boatman's Song* they did 'in dreams behold the Hebrides'.

But there are dreams and dreams; there are those which leave but a vague impression on the mind, and there are those which haunt one with a peculiar force, which are full of detail and the fact of longing, longing which can possess one with the physical quality and strength of hunger or of thirst. It was this kind of dream, and not the vague maunderings of Celtic Twilight Sleep so fashionable at the end of last century, which possessed the exiled Highlander of a hundred, a hundred and fifty, two hundred years ago. It is this kind of dream that one can catch a hint of in his poems and speeches in exile.

Upon a fine June or October day one can stand upland and inland at some such spot as the head of Loch Hourn, or above Morar, and look out over the coloured hills and valleys below one, over the Western and inland sea to where the inner Hebrides seem to float like anchored ships upon the pellucid and unruffled ocean. At such a time and in such a place it is impossible to believe that for over a thousand years men could have been nurtured in such surroundings and not have been affected by them in some deeper way than merely in the effect of recognizing them and loving them as a part of their homeland. Not only is it impossible to believe this, but it is right and reasonable to perceive in the traditional character of the Western Highlander, in his customs, his legends, the impress of such scenes. At such times it is easy to see why the ancient Highlanders believed so intensely in *Tir nan og*, the islands of the blest, the land of eternal youth, which lay out in the ultimate West and beyond the furthest Hebrides. Nor is one's sympathy for his belief shaken by the bitter reflexion that many of his kind found the ultimate West in sorrow and in tears upon a barren shore and at the end of enforced emigration.

At such times, and in such places too, one can understand why the sensuous imagination of the old Gaelic poets was content merely to name the details rather than describe the quality of such a scene. The Western Highlands, though they have been the subject of much shocking art and sentimental writing, have been the despair of most true artists who have been allured by them into an attempt to express them. The elusive luminous Northern light has defeated the painters; and the strong yet indefinable atmosphere of this countryside, joyously beautiful and inescapably sad by turns, has defied the modern poets.

Perhaps there is one poem in English which catches something of the quality of the Highlands. But its subject was probably the Central Highlands and was certainly not the Western seaboard. It was a sudden and lyrical outburst; and its author did not attempt it again in verse. It was written some seventy years ago by a poet whose imaginative sympathy for the old pre-romantic Highland way of life is much evident in else that he wrote. He was nonetheless a romantic himself, but one who came too late and was too much of an artist to be affected by the sentimentalities of the later romantic school. Indeed, in many of his ways of thought he was almost of our own age – or so recent critics have recently been saying. The poem is to be found in many anthologies, and is well known; some indeed would consider it hackneyed. But it is difficult to think of any other writing in English, whether in verse or prose, which can convey so unmistakably that Highland sense of silence haunted by a thousand undertones of music, of space filled by a thousand details of form and colour. It is R. L. Stevenson's *In the Highlands* ...

> In the highlands, in the country places,
> Where the old plain men have rosy faces,
> And the young fair maidens
> Quiet eyes;
>
> Where essential silence chills and blesses,
> And for ever in the hill-recesses
> *Her* more lovely music
> Broods and dies –
>
> O to mount again where erst I haunted;
> Where the old red hills are bird-enchanted,
> And the low green meadows
> Bright with sward;

And when even dies, the million-tinted,
And the night has come, and planets glinted,
Lo, the valley hollow
Lamp-bestarr'd!

O to dream, O to awake and wander
There, and with delight to take and render
Through the trance of silence,
Quiet breath!

Lo! for there, among the flowers and grasses,
Only the mightier movement sounds and passes;
Only winds and rivers,
Life and death.

CHAPTER SIX

INDUSTRIAL SCOTLAND

THAT huge change in the life of the working and middle classes which we call the Industrial Revolution had in Scotland as large an effect as in England, but it was a different one – different in its origin, different in kind. In England the Industrial Revolution completely transformed the lives of millions of men and women in the Midlands and in the North. Some few benefited by this transformation, some, like the Lancashire cotton operatives, managed to carry over into their new existence the native gusto of their own personality, but for the large majority it was a violent, unnatural, and profound change that had been imposed upon them, often to the detriment of their character and always to the destruction of their natural way of life. In Scotland the Industrial Revolution, though quite as much of an upheaval, was in a sense a fulfilment.

When one looks at some of the outward and visible signs of the Industrial Revolution in Scotland this may seem a strange, a shocking, even a cynical word to use about it. One can well imagine the kind of questions that an incomer to modern Scotland might put if he heard the word fulfilment after his first sight of the Scottish industrial scene: Can these squalid mining towns and villages that succeed in making the already mournful landscape of Central Scotland even more depressing than Nature had intended it to be, those superfetating slums of Glasgow, Dundee, of parts of Edinburgh, and of the industrial

143

area of the South-West, and those other sullen little towns scattered elsewhere that once had a quality of their own and a place in Scottish history, but are now swept into the drab uniformity of industrialism – can these and many other shocking things (shocking not only to one's sense of beauty and fitness) be the signs of a national fulfilment in Scotland? Can the morose, grace-hating, or at least grace-fearing crowds of troglodytic men that pour out of the Moloch-mouthed temples of industry in the drizzle of week-day evenings or, at times of unemployment, stand in sad rings upon some sour derelict spot outside the town playing pitch and toss with a small boy posted to warn them of the approach of a policeman be really fulfilling themselves? Can their wives who become slatterns before thirty and their children savages before seven, who live in a slum atmosphere of squalor and gang warfare, be the products of a system of Scottish fulfilment? If so, it would have been better, one feels inclined to say, if Scotland had never fulfilled herself and had remained in a crude and primitive but at least not repellent state of expectancy.

To put this rhetorical question in this superficial way is, however, to beg it. For it is superficial to see only the ugly and shocking elements in the Scottish industrial scene. And however tempting it may be to pass judgement after the first shock of being exposed to that ugliness, especially if one comes from outside Scotland, one must consider other things, particularly the origin of industrialism in Scotland and its complete and not only its partial effects on the Scottish character.

But before doing even that the incomer should be careful not to confuse what was already in the Scottish character with what the Industrial Revolution has done to it.

The taciturnity, the gracelessness, the apparent morose-
ness, apparently relieved only by sardonic humour, of
many of the Scottish working men are, for instance, Scottish and Lowland characteristics – though industrialism
may have harshened them, made them more obvious.
Much also of the overpowering ugliness of the Scottish
industrial town is only an extension of that grim austerity
which you will find in small towns in the Lowlands whose
buildings have grown since the eighteenth century un-
touched by industrialism. And unspeakable though the
worst slums in the large cities may have been, and vile
though some of them may remain, are they not merely an
example of Scotland's habit of pushing things to extremes? And before passing judgement on what industrialism has done to the working-class family in Scotland one
should get to know them a little better than by watching
or listening in streets, at street corners, in public houses
and shops. One should see the men at work and the
women with their neighbours and at home. And one
should see them in holiday mood – 'doon the watter' on
Clyde steamer, at a football match, or in a music hall.

While it is true that one should certainly get to know a
little more about the Scottish working man than the average visitor to Glasgow or Dundee (even if that visitor
comes no further than from Edinburgh or the country)
before one criticizes on Scottish industrialism, there
is another element to be considered. For even when
one does get to know the Glasgow shipyard worker and
when one has learned to recognize and relish his qualities,
that will not explain the meaning of the statement that
the Industrial Revolution was in a sense a fulfilment in
Scotland. To do this one must look back to the state of
our country in the middle of the eighteenth century.

By 1750 something had occurred in Scotland which laid the way open to a change all over the country. That change would have taken place even if the Industrial Revolution had never arisen. This was the departure of the old way of life in Scotland which had lasted for centuries, but which was now disappearing, partly from political, partly from economic causes, and partly because the country was now opening herself to the world in a way that she had lost since the Reformation.

This disappearance of the old Scotland manifested itself in many ways. After the defeat of the Jacobite rising in 1745 the centuries-old Highland feudal system disappeared forever, and, the policy of enforced emigration apart, this radically changed the whole system of life in over half the geographical area of the country. It had its effects too South of the Highland line. The old, almost religious veneration for high birth received something of a shock right down to the English Border; and with the now all but universally accepted (if not welcomed) defeat of the last chance of Scotland regaining a Stuart King the Union with England in matters outside the law and the Church now rested on a firmer basis. It was more assured, more inevitable, whichever way you cared to look at it.

This, naturally, was a matter that caused much relief in the wealthier Glasgow circles, which had since the Union of the Parliaments been building up a prosperous trade with America, thus opening one more door between Scotland and the world. And so until the American war put a temporary stop to it, Glasgow commerce with the New World flourished, making not only Glasgow but to a certain extent all Scotland richer. This increased wealth began to make itself felt in mechanical and material ways before the first inventions of the Industrial Revolution had come to Scotland. Roads were improved beyond measure, communications of all kinds were established as they had never been before all over the kingdom, and with England. At the end of the seventeenth century it took fourteen days to travel between Edinburgh and London. James Boswell in 1762 did it in five, and according to his journal in tolerable comfort.

This increasingly settled state of affairs, along with the increasing wealth, encouraged men all over the country to take a longer view and to manage their business, including agriculture, according to modern methods. Large farms took the place of small ones, land that had hitherto been regarded as good for nothing would often be reclaimed and included in these larger farms which were now being run with a view to profit in the years to come, and not merely as immediate protection against winter starvation. With the high price of corn which obtained in the war years these new farmers soon made money and extended their improvements.

There was change also in the way of life in the social strata both above and below the new farmers. The great landlords who had escaped the charge of disaffection by being on the winning side in 1745 began to manage their estates in the modern manner, laying out their lands according to design, planting trees, and in general imitating the Southern tendency to look upon the hereditary ownership of land as a business rather than as a feudal position with duty and privilege attached to it. On the other hand, the poorer agricultural workers found their small lands often swallowed up with little or no warning in the creation of larger farms and lost their old independence. Uprooted, often resentful without being actively disaffected, they too were ripe for further changes.

Edinburgh, the Capital city of this small country that was now aligning itself with the modern Europe of the late eighteenth century, did not at first enjoy or suffer from these material changes. But she did undergo a revolution of the spirit and mind which was quite as striking as the changes that were occurring elsewhere throughout the country, and which was in its own kind as characteristic of the new age in Scotland.

Edinburgh's celebrated intellectual and to a lesser degree artistic efflorescence, which occurred in the eighteenth century, beginning with the rise to fame of Adam Smith and David Hume and ending and culminating with Walter Scott, made all Europe conscious of Scotland and her Capital as it had never been before. If in the ill-fated reign of James IV the first stirrings of the springtime of Edinburgh's cultural life began to make themselves felt, only to be blasted at Flodden, here was a long-delayed high summer; but as with natural summers it bore within it the germ of autumn. While it is true that this period brought Edinburgh to a position which gained her the name of 'the Academy of Europe', and opened her gates to the world, it also sapped at the foundations of her nationality.

Edinburgh in the second half of the eighteenth century was the intellectual superior of London. 'I can stand,' said the enthusiastic Englishman Amyat, 'at the Mercat Cross of Edinburgh, and within half an hour I can shake by the hand fifty men of genius.' Maybe. But it is a discouraging thought for the Edinburgh patriot to reflect on how many of these 'men of genius' were taking lessons in the 'correct speaking of English', were apeing London manners and deliberately expelling Scotticisms from their way of thought and behaviour as well as from their speech. With the two outstanding exceptions of Robert Burns and Walter Scott the great men of this period in Scottish literature and thought were less consciously Scottish than their kind were before, or indeed have been since.

These changes which had come about in urban and rural Scotland, in Edinburgh and Glasgow, as well as in the smaller towns and in the countryside, made Scotland peculiarly ripe for some new development. And that development soon proclaimed itself in the Industrial Revolution.

The always inquisitive and acquisitive Scottish mind took to the industrial inventions which reached them from across the Border with a triple gusto. It took to them because they were new, and it was avid for new things. It took to them because they came from the outside world (in this instance England); and it took to them because of its talent for practical invention was large, and at this period active.

The Industrial Revolution, having penetrated from the southern kingdom into this new Scotland, already in the melting pot of change, was not only seized upon with delight and hope but was improved upon. The spirit of adventure which in the world of philosophy and political economy animated Hume and Adam Smith, or, in Romance, Walter Scott, impelled James Watt to invent the steam engine and Henry Bell the steam-driven boat. It also inspired experiment and invention in many smaller ways among names less known to us now in such fields as the weaving of cloth and the manufacture of domestic goods.

But it was in the heavy industries employing coal and iron that the commercial talent, one might almost say the genius, of the Scot of this new age discovered itself with speed, and to the accompaniment of considerable gusto on the part of those who possessed it and practised it. Scotland had amongst her natural resources both coal and iron; but the coal was not of the coking standard of that in England and Wales. And so at first she was handicapped in the use of her own material. The ingenuity of her inventors of industry, however, came to her rescue. When Mushet discovered the high grade of ore in blackband ironstone, which had been up till then neglected though present in large quantities in Scotland, and when Neilson later invented the hot-blast furnace which made easy the smelting of blackband, Scotland had full access to the philosopher's stone of the nineteenth century – iron. Glasgow trade with the Western world had been established well before the Industrial Revolution. But now the men of that revolution lent their skill and their services to the enlargement and enrichment of Scotland's largest and richest town. They dredged, deepened, and made navigable the river Clyde up to the heart of Glasgow, thus characteristically of their age, kind, and nation, taking advantage of one of Scotland's most important natural assets, and improving upon it.

Coal, iron, and the Clyde – these were the foundations of the Scotland that was to emerge from the ferment of the ending of the eighteenth century. From the time of Neilson's momentous discovery each new invention, each piece of good fortune, led to another. The new railways, annually spreading their networks all over Great Britain, demanded iron and the skill to fashion that iron: Scotland had both. The export of pig iron called for ships to send it abroad. The new ships were now fitted with steam engines. Once again Scotland provided the skill in the building of engines and the material from which they were made. And when finally there began to float upon the seas of the world ships that were heavier than water, the iron and the skill to make them existed superabundantly in Scotland. Nor was this all. In the long reaches of the Clyde just West of Glasgow there was the ideal waterway on which these incredible new monsters of the nineteenth century could be built and launched. The age of Scotland's mightiest and most passionately pursued industry, that of shipbuilding, had begun. It was an age and an industry that fashioned our country's destinies until the first World War.

The Industrial Revolution was therefore in its own dark yet deep and vital way a fulfilment of Scotland's destiny and needs at a time when from the deep change in her, the deep calling upon her hidden strength of the past, the deep looking into her future she was clamant for fulfilment. The 'dark Satanic mills' which arose so remorselessly in the North of England changed the face of the countryside and enslaved millions of English men, women, and children; but they were the outward signs of something that had for the most part been imposed upon England. In Scotland the iron-smelting furnaces that glowed in orange and vermilion against the long and sombre Lowland winter nights, the coal mines that ever further and more darkly burrowed beneath the Lowland surfaces, and above all the great clanging shipyards of the Clyde had been conceived and born by Scotland herself.

The large wealth that poured into our small country was naturally, and according to the *laissez faire* politics of the time, concentrated in the hands of a small minority of the population. Great families, the names of some of which are still a power in the land, arose to positions in which they could control not only the wealth of Scotland but the destinies of many of their countrymen. But these families, particularly in Glasgow and the West, were continually changing in status and were, with the increasing wealth of the country, having their numbers added to, sometimes from those who had started in the humblest circumstances. Ambition therefore animated all classes. And with the examples before them of men who in boyhood had walked the streets of Glasgow barefoot, but who were now captains of industry, even the poorest industrial workers in that time of ferment could, if they had determination as well as imagination, dream their dreams of sharing in their country's wealth.

There was another reason why a large number of those hundreds of thousands of Scots working men who from the Highlands and the Lowlands, from the Border Hills, and some even from the Hebrides poured into the basins of the Clyde and the Forth, did not consider themselves hopelessly enslaved as did so many of their kind who were caught up in the Industrial Revolution in other countries. This reason came from a combination of elements in the Scottish character.

The most important was one which was shared by both Lowlander and Highlander. This was their love of craftsmanship and their pride in expressing themselves as craftsmen. There were superb qualities which showed themselves in the structure, one might almost say the life, of those ships made and launched upon the Clyde in the nineteenth century. These qualities remain, so that even to-day 'Clyde-built' are the last words of praise that can be bestowed upon any boat in any harbour in the world. The science of the last century and the wealth of the last century working together in organization upon the natural resources of Scotland did not alone produce the qualities of 'Clyde-built'. There was another and equally important element which was in its own way a natural resource of Scotland – the craftsmanship of the Clyde worker.

To those who think of craftsmanship as something connected only with the making of small and domestic objects it may seem strange to use the word about the construction of a giant liner in the Clyde. Anyone who knows the sea would smile at such a notion; for he knows that these boats, great and small, are from bow to stern examples of pure craftsmanship. Even a man who as a passenger, with little knowledge of boat construction and less of navigation, travels the seas in a Clyde-built ship, if he has any imagination as well as power of observation, will surely feel this too. In a hundred details that make themselves manifest to him each new day at sea, as well as in the whole shape, the large majestic fact of the ship itself, he will perceive that she is a work of art that has come out of more than the mind of one designer, that has been made by hundreds upon hundreds of patient pairs of hands used by craftsmen.

This love of craftsmanship, the evidences of which you will find in the detail as well as in the whole of any typically Scottish industrial product, is one of the most important things to recognize in the Scottish working man. Unlike many other industrial workers, he can really love his job; for it has given him an outlet for something that is fundamental in his character. It has been said earlier that this something is shared both by the Lowlander and the Celt. The Lowlander whose ancestors struggled with the harsh land of Scotland's farms relishes the struggle with machinery. The native austerity in him relishes too the austere duty of producing the best mechanical job he can with the forces of matter at his command. He loves conquering as a craftsman and a workman the great work on hand with which he is engaged along with so many other workmen.

The Highlander has traditionally loved to exercise his ingenuity in exquisitely detailed work produced by his hands. Ancient as well as comparatively modern Celtic art shows this in the endless and intricate patterns which the Celt has always loved and which he has been so patiently adept at producing. It is perhaps not too fanciful to see in the craftsmanship of shipbuilding and other smaller but characteristic industries of the Clyde an outlet for this deep instinct of the Celtic Highlanders who made up a considerable part of the Scottish immigrants into the industrial belt a hundred and fifty years ago.

Then there was another element in the character of the Scottish worker of the industrial period which helped to prevent him from feeling a slave. The iron and steel age was for all Scotland of the time a challenge, and a challenge to those fighting qualities in the Scot of all classes and conditions which had so long been dissipated in useless quarrels or expended and lost in causes which seemed from their beginning to be doomed to failure. This was a challenge which again appealed to the Lowlander as well as to the Highlander; and if the Lowlander answered it with a grim determination, and the Celt with a fiery imagination, their objects were the same, and at last they found themselves allies in the same cause – and at last too, it seemed, a cause in which they could triumph.

The Scottish Lowlander and the Scottish Celt felt then that with the arrival of the Industrial Revolution in the country which they shared they were faced with an heroic struggle worthy of their combined efforts, the combined efforts of Scotsmen of different race but one nation now united. The Celt would not have been a Celt and the Lowlander not a Lowlander if this combination in these circumstances had not given their joint struggle with the opportunities of the new age a romantic, even an aesthetic and a religious quality. The aesthetic and romantic side of the heroic age of Scottish industry is expressed in the craftsmanship of the early shipbuilders, whose beautifully designed craft sailed out from the dark, romantic waters of the Clyde into the beauty of that river's estuary, and thus to the ultimate ports of the habitable globe. And that many of the craftsmen of the Clyde did (with the utmost outward reserve) think of their work in this way there can be no doubt. The religious and powerfully philosophic impetus which, equally without doubt, affected the Lowland cast of thought amongst the industrial workers has never been better expressed than in Kipling's *McAndrew's Hymn*.

Kipling, that half-English half-Scottish Anglo-Indian, was the product of the Victorian British Empire at the height of its most powerful and romantic period. He drew his inspiration from a hundred sources in that great time of which he was the child. His genius, devoted to no one element in it, could interpret any one of those individuals who expressed those different elements which caught his fancy, Tommy Atkins, the Indian fakir, the Sussex peasant, the Cockney, the Scottish engineer, he could speak for all and each of these component parts of the Victorian British Empire of which he was the most eloquent voice.

He could put their own thoughts into their own mouths and make them speak in words which they would never have brought out for themselves, but which nevertheless were their own words authentically distilled from their own essence. In this vein it is doubtful if he surpassed *McAndrew's Hymn*. No Scottish engineer ever spoke like McAndrew in prose, let alone verse, but many engineers who went out from the Clyde to sail the seven seas, as well as many of those who stayed behind to build the vessels which carried Glasgow's name to the farthest parts of the earth, may have thought these thoughts:

Lord, Thou hast made this world below the shadow of a dream,
An', taught by time, I tak' it so – exceptin' always Steam.
From coupler-flange to spindle-guide I see Thy Hand, O God –
Predestination in the stride o' yon connectin'-rod.
John Calvin might ha' forged the same – enorrmous, certain,
 slow –
Ay, wrought it in the furnace-flame – *my* 'Institutio'.

. . . . .

Romance! Those first-class passengers they like it very well,
Printed and bound in little books; but why don't poets tell?
I'm sick of all their quirks an' turns – the loves an' doves they
 dream –
Lord, send a man like Robbie Burns to sing the Song o' Steam!
To match wi' Scotia's noblest speech yon orchestra sublime
Whaurto – uplifted like the Just – the tail-rods mark the time.
The crank-throws give the double-bass, the feed-pumps sobs
 an' heaves,
An' now the main eccentrics start their quarrel on the sheaves:
Her time, her own appointed time, the rocking link-head bides,
Till – hear that note? – the rod's return whings glimmerin'
 through the guides.*

* These lines from *McAndrew's Hymn* are taken from 'The Seven Seas', and are quoted by permission of Mrs George Bambridge, of Doubleday and Co. Inc., and of the Macmillan Co. of Canada Ltd.

'Lord, send a man like Robbie Burns to sing the Song
' Steam!' There speaks the industrial Scottish craftsman
f the nineteenth century filled not only with the glory of
he struggle, and the religious sense in that struggle, but
vith the feeling that all this was somehow bound up in
·cotland.

Men such as these, living in the fullness of the new age
f iron, steel, and industrial craftsmanship, the new age
vhich their country and they had done so much to create,
lid not think of themselves as slaves, nor had their fore-
athers in the wars of independence or later in the Cove-
·ant armies, or later still when some of them had strug-
·led in the faint hope of keeping alive the old Gaelic way
·f life. But all that had been a long time ago, and in the
·nterval, the long and depressing interval, the Scot had
·een thwarted of his passion to work for and fight in a
·ause in which he believed, which was his own. To many
·n Scotland the Industrial Revolution came at long last as
·uch a cause. To them truly it was a fulfilment.

Fulfilment though it may have been, the Industrial
Revolution in Scotland, as elsewhere, brought many
·orrors with it. It is characteristic of Scotland that these
·orrors, growing and existing alongside the genuine pas-
·ion and idealism of the new age, should have been partic-
·larly horrible. No slums in Europe were more squalid,
·nore wretched, more infernal than those which sprung up
·n Glasgow and the West in the middle of the nineteenth
·entury. And by an odd freak of sympathy Edinburgh,
·hough much less influenced by industrialism, succeeded in
·urning her Old Town into a slum that was nearly as bad.
·hese slums, into which sank those human by-products
·f the industrial age that could not take advantage of
·he rising tide (including many pathetic remnants of the

foreign invasion that had been lured into Scotland by dreams of prosperity or driven out of their own countries by famine), were breeding grounds of poverty, disease and crime. A new class of poor people more utterly impoverished, more wretched and—and this was important—more outlawed from the prosperous society around them than at any time in the history of Scotland grew up in the towns, in Dundee in the East, in the smaller industrial towns of the Central plain as well as in Glasgow and the West.

This outlawed, reckless, and often rootless society which with the evidences of human misery that it produced made, if possible, even more ugly the ugliness of the Scottish industrial scene, produced political consequences. Though most of its number (being rootless) were too hopeless to fight their misery by positive action and only sought escape from it by the anodynes of drink, methylated spirits, and the like, their plight aroused sympathy and indignation amongst all classes. This sympathy and indignation was the origin of the Labour movement in Scotland which embraced such diverse figures as Keir Hardie, the Scottish working man, and Cunninghame Graham, the most picturesquely Scottish aristocrat within living memory.

Cunninghame Graham, if not the only representative of his rank in the Scottish Labour movement, was sufficiently pre-eminent to stand alone in his kind. Keir Hardie was remarkable and distinctive enough to be, even in his class of sturdy individuals, outstanding. But between the two of them these two unusual men were characteristic of the Labour movement which had its beginnings in the Clyde basin in Scotland in the last century, that movement which has been responsible for the legend of the

'Red Clyde' which has obtained so long in the South and in other parts of Scotland. That this legend is exaggerated (indeed even false if one uses the term 'red' in the accepted modern sense) is clear if one looks at the Labour movement to-day in industrial Scotland and if one troubles to examine the origins from which it sprang.

The Labour movement, even in the worst slum districts of nineteenth-century Scotland, was not primarily based on the bitter anger, the jealousy, the understandably destructive rage of the miserable. Rather it was founded on indignation and compassion. It did not, therefore, as did similar movements of the oppressed on the Continent, lead naturally to that form of totalitarianism, the 'dictatorship of the proletariat', which is what most people mean by 'red' politics to-day. No one would have been more repelled by the slave state of the extreme left as we know it in parts of Europe to-day than Cunninghame Graham or Keir Hardie. Nor would these two exceptional men have been alone in this feeling of repulsion. Though he may have worked in batches of many hundreds on great enterprises and for great firms, the Scottish industrial worker throughout the last century remained true to his nationally essential individuality. The Clyde and other industrial districts of Scotland may have been the nurseries of Radicalism, Socialism, and other movements for freedom throughout the Victorian era, but freedom and individuality remained for those who struggled in these movements the operative words.

They still are so to-day. And that is why, despite the full misery of unemployment between the wars, despite the admixture of foreign blood which might have introduced a more foreign concept of the revolution of the left, the Communists have been consistently disappointed in what they have long looked upon as one of the most potentially fruitful soils for their gospel in Great Britain, the industrial districts of Scotland. They have, of course, made their conquests and conversions in the 'red Clyde' district, but these have been mostly amongst the incomers and traditionally dispossessed rather than the native Scots. The intractable Scottish love of individuality in the still dominant Scottish number of working men in the Clyde district and the West has up to the present proved too strong for them.

That this independence, this strong sense of individuality in the Scottish industrial worker has survived the depression and disasters of the last thirty years at all, let alone so well, is remarkable. For with the ending of the first World War a succession of blows were struck at the trade of Scotland which all but deprived her of the benefits which she had gained from the Industrial Age without getting rid of its evil effects. From the 1920's onwards the thing that the Industrial Revolution had done for Scotland began to be destroyed. The outside world, which from Waterloo until the outbreak of the first World War had been an ever-increasing market for the kind of heavy goods of industry which Scotland produced, suddenly began to need them no more. Foreign countries were learning to make these goods for themselves, and though they were inferior to the standard of 'Clyde-built' they were satisfied with them. Steam too, which had demanded the use of the kind of material which Scotland produced and fashioned, began to be superseded by other motive powers, the internal combustion engine and electricity. A new economy also was springing up in the outer world which demanded from mechanical craftsmen, and in

mense numbers, such small and everyday things as
dio sets, bicycles, vacuum cleaners, motor cars, and the
e which could be produced easily and efficiently in the
nglish Midlands, not to mention in countries across the
as.

As the great industries of the Clyde and the West
clined, it must have been a bitter reflection for some of
ose who suffered to think that it was the inventiveness
d the ingenuity of individual Scots in the fields of elec-
icity and other branches of the new science that was
priving so many of their countrymen of their livelihood.
nd if it seem strange now that these same Scots, whose
thers and grandfathers had so eagerly exploited the
ventions of the last century, could not adapt themselves
make use of the inventions of Bell and Baird as well as
any of their lesser known compatriots who had done so
uch pioneer work in radio and the telephone, in the
uilding of motor cars, we must take into account their
aracter and temperament, which had built the Indus-
ial Revolution. That character had hurled the Scots into
e huge struggle of the heavy industry with such momen-
m that the momentum itself could not be easily deflect-
d into diverse and lesser channels. It was no good.
ou could not turn McAndrew of Kipling's Hymn from
eing the servant (and the lord) of steam and steel and
on into a petrol motor mechanic or a radio engineer
vernight.

The great industrial depression then which between
he wars affected all Great Britain and which caused such
itiable misery in Lancashire and other parts of England
ounded Scotland not only economically but in her
ational pride. Clyde-built goods (and this applied not
nly to ships) remained in their own kind as excellent as

anything that you could find in the world, but the wor
no longer wanted them. Scottish industry, which h;
prided itself on two things, the first-class quality of
production and the fact that it was in the forefront
industrial progress and achievement, now found itself ou
moded, and by industries that it despised. The affront w
deep.

The affront was deeply felt, and by all classes in Sco
tish industry. Innumerable McAndrews as well as 'S
Kenneth' (in Kipling's poem the Chairman of the shi]
ping line) were mortified and puzzled by the turn even
had taken. Their pride of craftsmanship was hu
and their patriotism wounded in its tenderest part. An
maybe it is not too fanciful to say that there d
scended on them something of the bitterness of th
Covenanter who had seen the world 'whüring afte
strange Gods'.

Hurt pride, wounded patriotism: these were not a
they had to suffer. There was also the shocking economi
effects of the depression and the painful state of min
produced by those effects. Anyone who lived in Scotlanc
who travelled at all in the country in the 1920's and '30'
will not forget the sullen misery of hundreds of thousand
of some of the finest industrial craftsmen in the world, wh
now found themselves idle. The grey skies of the Scottis]
winter, the grim industrial countryside with the grea
hills above and behind it, and the grey sea at its gates
those skies and that countryside which had once seemec
to provide a sombre but suitable, almost majestic, back
ground for Scotland's Titanic struggle with the new ag
of industry, now combined to make a huge amphitheatr
in which was played a tragedy of poverty, squalor, anc
creeping inanition. As one observed it one felt at time

that one was witnessing another episode in Scottish history similar to the tragedy of the Highland evictions. There was the same mass deprivation of the power of life imposed from without. There were, however, two differences. The Highlands had been deserted. The Clyde Valley was not. The Highlands remained beautiful. Industrial Scotland became more ugly.

Never indeed had the industrial scene in Scotland appeared so ugly – spiritually as well as physically. What had been grim became merely squalid, what had been austere became meanly poor. The slums where once a kind of fierce if degraded life had existed amongst the lower ranks of those who lived upon the fringes of the great industrial movement now sank into a crapulous decay even more decadent than their earlier state. Those who passed some kind of existence in them, whether descendants of the imported Irish or of the native Scots, now not only had no work, but, it seemed, no hope of any. There were now denied them even those occasional outbursts of sporadic prosperity which had enabled the more feckless of them to escape the ugliness of their world in drink. More and more they were driven to exert their pathetic ingenuity in the invention of the cheaper anodynes such as the drinking of methylated spirit, or of furniture polishes through which gas from the bracket on the stair-head had been passed.

The housing position, always bad throughout a hundred years of industrialism, now became all but desperate. With the slowing down, the near stopping of the great machine which this multitude served as well as created, which up to a point had served them with the means of life, there was no new building, no new accommodation of any kind. And yet their families increased.

If there was not also an increase in crime and physical savagery, it was only because these poor people, abandoned by the industrial machine and deprived even of the chance of struggling for their livelihood, were too enfeebled to exert themselves by violence.

Apart from the human scene, the physical aspect of industrial Scotland became more and more sad and depressing. The silent shipyard, the deserted pit-heads, the decrepit and obviously moribund little industrial towns all added their touch of misery to the already grim scene. Chesterton, no friend, to put it mildly, of the Great Britain created by the Industrial Revolution, has described his impressions of a demoniac energy illuminated by the fairy lights of the lamps on the miners' caps when he visited South-Western Scotland in the Edwardian era. Had he come twenty years later he would have found little energy, demonaic or angelic, and would have seen few miners' caps twinkling through the gloom of a winter's night.

The ugliness and depressing quality of the industrial scene in Scotland must, even in the last century when things were going well, have been severe and impressive. The ugliness and depression during the period of mass unemployment and in the first wave of the realization that the age of Scotland's coal and iron and steel had passed was overpowering.

It was this ugliness and depression which during two decades most impressed itself in the eye of the visitor. It was this that was responsible for the kind of scenes described at the beginning of this chapter which to the observer seemed to make it shocking and cynical to talk of the Industrial Revolution in Scotland as being in one sense a fulfilment.

Yet through all this there remained one thing not quite destroyed. That was a hard intractable quality in the character of the majority of the native Scots working people caught in this disaster. This was a quality which had existed over the centuries. It had endured, conquered, and suffered defeat in many struggles. Above all, just before the iron and coal age it had been thwarted so that some thought that it had been softened; but it had not. And now, when a more sudden, a more dramatic disaster threatened it, it was not obliterated. When during the latter part of these two decades there came the rare opportunity to build the two great ocean liners, the 'Queen Mary' and the 'Queen Elizabeth', it was discovered that the men who built them had not lost their craftsmanship nor their fervour in work.

They had indeed not lost that fervour; rather it had grown in them silently and deeply in the long and thwarted years to burst out again in a form both dramatic and touching. No one who was present in Clydebank on the day they started on the 'Queen Mary' after the 'long lay-off' will easily forget the sight of those grey streets in the early morning. ... *The men were running to their work.*

In the impetus of industry during the last war this quality remained; though those who possessed it could not help feeling that conditions were unnatural and not likely to last. Now some years after the war has ended that impetus still continues, and unemployment is not nearly so rife as in the 1920's and '30's. But what of the future? No one can tell. Nor would it be proper in a conspectus of the Scottish people as they are to-day (such as this book is intended to be) to put forward guesses and prophecies.

Two things, however, are certain. The first is that the

old grim glory is gone – the glory of the earlier struggle when it seemed that out of her own character as well as out of her own natural materials Scotland would forever be pouring out to the world the fruits of her conquest of the industrial age; for that age in its old form has gone too. The second is that that character, as it exists in the working people of Scotland, remains and survives as it has remained and survived in the past.

What is he like, the Scottish industrial working man? The present writer feels a reluctance in attempting to answer this question. He cannot pretend that he is as familiar with the Clyde workers as he is with others of his countrymen, the rural Lowlanders of the Borders and the North-East, the Highlanders and Islanders, both Celtic and Norse, and above all the citizens of all kinds and classes that come from Edinburgh. This familiarity with his native city, the very fact that he is a native of it does indeed only increase his reluctance to be heard on the subject of the Clyde worker. Moreover, as he has lived for a year or two at different times in Glasgow and enjoyed (always as an inquisitive stranger) its diverse vitality, he has learned one thing: – it is highly dangerous to generalize about, even to attempt to describe the characteristics of, so individual a people as the workers in the Clyde basin. He has heard too the sardonic comments from some of these workers on those who in print or in public speech have tried to define their characteristics. The thought of this book finding its way into the hands of a Scottish industrial worker from the West and the comments (or the more awful silence) that might ensue when he reaches these pages makes the present writer even more hesitant.

However, there is no doubt but that the Clyde worker

as certain general characteristics; and these can sometimes be seen quite clearly from without – even by someone who comes from Edinburgh. This, in brief, is how
they appear to such an observer.

The century of industrial struggle has, while animating
him with a purpose, underlined his Scottish Lowland
qualities of sardonic taciturnity, especially when brought
face to face with foreigners; that is, anyone who comes
from a different background or who has markedly different values. On the other hand the vitality, the large
communal nature of that struggle conducted in crowded
and urban circumstances (combined possibly with the
presence of Celtic blood in him) has given him, when
amongst his own kind, a liveliness faintly, but only faintly,
akin to the Cockney spirit.

You may feel the full shock of his sardonic taciturnity if
you get into conversation with him in a railway carriage
and say something that he disagrees with. You will
also feel the exhilaration of his liveliness if you go to a
football match which he is attending in large numbers, to
a Glasgow music hall or, as has already been mentioned
in these pages, if you go with him and his family 'doon
the watter' on a Clyde pleasure steamer. You will appreciate his liveliness in its homelier or more domestic side
only if you are fortunate enough to be received into his
house. You may get some idea of it, however, in the pages
of J. J. Bell's *Wee MacGregor*, or some of John Buchan's
novels, in Neil Munro, and should you have listened to
the Scottish Home Service of the B.B.C. in the last ten
years, in that highly popular series of broadcasts about a
Glasgow working-class family, *The McFlannels*.

The mention of *The McFlannels* reminds one of an element that exists in some of the Glasgow and West of

Scotland working classes which is not often remarked upon – intense respectability. This element in the McFlannel broadcasts is admittedly laid on with a trowel so that it is to some listeners who have, almost against their own inclinations, become McFlannel addicts repellent, if not quite incredible. No one in the McFlannel family, no one in their circle, not even those to whom the family are hostile, who are held up for our ridicule and contempt ever drinks, smokes, goes to the theatre, the music hall, a public meeting, or a political gathering. If any of them have ever shown consciousness of the fact that the cinema exists, the present writer has not caught them at it. Love of a very diluted and frustrating kind does occasionally enter into their domestic story, but it has no passion in it, and seems remote even from anything so practical and fleshly as mating. Indeed, so free of all carnal desires do the McFlannels seem that one wonders how anyone in their circle is ever conceived and born. And all this, if you please, takes place in the home of a Glasgow riveter in some teeming crowded district such as Maryhill, with its flaring Saturday night pubs and its all-the-week flaring cinemas.

This respectability of these bodiless creations of the wireless is, of course, exaggerated, but it is an exaggeration of a truth; and that it is a truth is testified to in the extreme popularity of the broadcasts in Glasgow itself. The truth is that even in the poorest Glasgow families, those who have suffered most deeply from the industrial depression, who must have constantly been exposed to the temptation to 'forget it all' in drink, or in anything else that comes along handy, there often exists a hard and intractable core of decent, heroic respectability. This respectability may not push itself to such ridiculous extremes as in the McFlannels, but it does discover itself in the thrift, the self-restraint, the strong family loyalty and other sturdy virtues which many a Glasgow family has inherited from its Lowland forebears.

That there is a less respectable side to the Scottish industrial worker the world well knows. Popular writers and popular comedians have seen to that. The drunken Glasgow working man is a familiar figure in fiction, journalism, and on the music hall stage. And no one would attempt to deny that the worker of the industrial belt is fond, over fond, of whisky when he can get it. Even nowadays, when the price of Scotland's national drink is extortionate, the drunkenness in Glasgow and the industrial towns on high days and holidays is obviously greater and obviously more passionately indulged in than anywhere else in Great Britain. Before the 1914 war, when the price of a bottle was three shillings, sometimes less, it is said that the sight of Argyle Street on a Saturday night was something one never forgot.

It is easy for the observer from gentler and sunnier climates, from less obviously austere circumstances, to account for this strong taste for drink by saying that it is the Scottish industrial worker's only escape from the ugliness and depression of his surroundings. There is naturally some truth in this, especially when one considers the worst slums where the worst misery occurs. But it is by no means the only reason; for by no means all of those who when they 'get a couple of drinks on a Saturday night' find that 'Glasgow belongs to them' do find the circumstances of industrial Scotland so ugly or depressing. Very few of them would exchange the Clyde in Glasgow for the Mediterranean or the shores of the Riviera. Many a regular Glasgow drinker who makes the night loud with the enjoyment of his potations drinks not so much to escape his surroundings as to enjoy them. They are a passionate people and take a passionate and even a positive pleasure in their drinking. They are individuals too, and find in the permitted saturnalia of drinking amongst their own class and kind a way of releasing their own individuality without inhibition.

This triumphant attitude of mind is triumphantly expressed in the words of the never to be sufficiently lamented late Will Fyffe:

> I belong to Glasgow,
> Dear old Glasgow town.
> There's nothing the matter wi' Glasgow
> Though it's going roun' an' roun'.
> I'm only a common old workin' chap
> As anyone here can see,
> But when I get a couple o' drinks on a Saturday night
> Glasgow belongs to me.

And having used this great comedian's verse, let us not forget his prose. The patter to this same song used to contain one highly revealing reflection, 'I cannae stand teetotallers. If you're teetotal you get an awful feeling that everybody's your boss.' There speaks the Scottish industrial worker from the depths of his individualistic soul and in the full flood of his alcoholic release.

There have been many admirable sketches of the 'type' in fiction and in journalism. The Glasgow stage and the Scottish wireless have often presented him effectively and truly. But the best writing about him is contained in that classic of the Clyde, *Glasgow in 1901*, written in that year for the contemporary Glasgow exhibition by three pseudonymous young Glasgow journalists who have since become famous. Anyone who ventures to write on the

Scottish industrial worker even to-day cannot but be conscious of how little he can add to this large achievement, and indeed how little the 'type' has changed in essentials in fifty years. Short of advising the reader to undertake the almost impossible task of obtaining a copy of this book (the fact that there has been no reprint since the early years of this century is a standing rebuke to Glasgow publishers), he can but point out how these essentials have remained, remained after the passing of half a century, after two wars and a major depression lasting for the best part of twenty years.

How true still are these remarks chosen nearly at random from the chapter on 'The Working Man' in *Glasgow in 1901* : –

'He is of the middle height and strongly built, and spare. His legs have not the robustness of the countryman's, but are wiry, and suit well his body. His face has harsh features which give it character; his forehead has prominent bones, his cheeks are fallen in, and the lines from his nose to his mouth are strongly marked. ... His fingers, broad and short, are those of a clever workman. ...'

'He is intelligent and has a clear perception of injustice. But according to his lights he is a reasonable man. He stauns up for himsel' not only against the common enemy his employer, but against his comrades in allied trades, if they invade his frontiers. ...'

'Of servility he has not a trace, "Sir" is an unknown word to him, "Thank you" an unknown phrase. He is the perfect type of "Wha daur meddle wi' me". ...'

'He can be brilliantly indecent, and will argue upon abstract points, and quibble with an indefatigable zeal. ...'

'He has grown to take his pleasures fiercely. ...'

'At bottom he is a very decent fellow. ... He has in him

much gracious humanity, which kindly influences would bring to flower.... He is good to his weans in a shamefaced way, but is not a demonstrative father, for he will usually introduce wee Hughie and wee Maggie to a stranger as "this yin and yon yin"....'

'Then there is one of an older type who seems to have adapted himself more perfectly to the conditions of his existence. ... He does not need the excitement for which the other craves and so does not care for football or whisky. His interest in argument is not less keen, but his discussions are political or theological. He is radical and Calvinist by inheritance and tradition, and though his active interest in Calvinism may have abated, its principles still control his conduct.... He is the backbone of the working classes, but though he is above the ruck he does not change its character. ...'

All this is still true to-day, fifty years later on. But events that have happened in those fifty years have discovered in the Glasgow working man qualities which were always there but which not everyone once recognized so clearly as they do now. We always suspected that he was 'a bonny fechter'. But it required two of the greatest wars in history to show exactly how bonny a fechter was the stocky little soldier of the Glasgow regiment. We always knew that he was built of durable stuff that he had acquired from his ancestors and had rendered more durable by his own struggles, that he was tenacious of his own values and his own self-respect. But exactly how durable and how tenacious he was we did not realize until he had passed through the twenty years of depression and unemployment that separated one great war from the other.

CHAPTER SEVEN

THE ISLANDS

THERE are seven hundred and eighty-seven islands around the coasts of Scotland. The compilers of the official Gazetteer from which this figure is taken defined an island not by its size, but expressed themselves in more practical terms. They decided that a Scottish island was any piece of solid land within the orbit of Scottish law, surrounded at all tides by sea water yet never submerged by it, either inhabited by man or growing sufficient vegetation perennially to support one or more sheep. This seemingly punctilious definition of so obvious a thing as an island was apparently necessary when describing a country so fretted, so eaten into by the sea, so surrounded by large and small archipelagoes as is Scotland. At any rate it is a definition which will suit our purpose here. Skerryvore, the remote Atlantic rock on which the lighthouse keeper and his staff live all the year round, thus qualifies as a Scottish island; so equally does the even more remote St Kilda, which is now desolate of humanity, but which has enough vegetation to support many sheep.

Of the remaining seven hundred and eighty-five islands that pertain to Scotland nearly all do support sheep at various seasons of the year; and some hundred and sixty are inhabited by man. In some of these the population amounts to several thousands, in others it has sunk to below twenty. In all of them the writ of Scottish law runs, and they are the largest number of islands under the jurisdiction of any one country in Europe. It is as if Scotland, herself so tantalizingly near to being an island, had conceived and born these archipelagoes out of her own body parthenogenetically and in recompense for having herself missed that happy state.

It may well be understood then that these islands have played and continue to play an important part in the life of their parent kingdom. It would be a mistake, however, to suppose that this is so only because they are so many or because they make up a considerable proportion of the land of Scotland. Historically they have been important to the country in the intermittent but constantly recurring warfare which she waged in her early centuries with her Northern neighbours. They were projections of herself which the Norse invaders could seize to her imminent peril; and in the long run when they were regained they became bastions of strength – outposts against the same enemy. Because of this outpost character, this exposed position, they were at first the source from which new and refreshing blood flowed into the body of Scotland.

Later when peace came to them they ceased to be perilous outposts against an enemy over the seas, and now, because of their remoteness, their *rôle* was reversed. They became the repositories of the old way of life in Scotland. And despite increasing hardships often imposed upon them politically and economically their inhabitants were able to preserve with a proud tenacity, rather than with a mere peasant obstinacy, their old customs, their old beliefs, and their old way of thought, language, and behaviour. Even now when this tenacity has had to face and, in some islands, to succumb to economic attack more severe than anything they knew before, the islanders of the West and the North in their differing ways remain the living guardians of much of our Scottish past – enisled not only in the seas but in the more cruel circumstance of time.

That they were isolated and tenacious of the past did not, however, mean that the main body of Scotland was cut off from their influence. The human contribution of the islands to Scotland has for two centuries been constant and quietly effective. No one who has lived and worked in Scotland can be unaware of this influence in religion, politics, in the general Scottish attitude towards life and, more remotely, in literature and song. Perhaps not more than one in ten people living on the mainland have visited any but the more immediate and holiday islands, but for those who are consciously Scottish Scotland without the Hebrides or the Norse Islands would be unthinkable; it would not be Scotland.

There are many who would agree to this who themselves have not been consciously influenced by the islands, who have met only one or two islanders on the mainland. They would agree because the fact of Scotland's islands will have impressed itself on to their minds since childhood. The maps that hung upon the walls of their schoolrooms, maps that show the scattered thrust of the Hebrides to the West and the sword-like gesture of Shetland to the North, the stories of the islands that are part of the legend of Scotland, the mere fact of their fascinatingly large number will have constantly reminded any Scottish child of them. And if that child has any imagination it cannot but be stirred by the romance of what he sees printed in crude colours upon his schoolroom maps – the romance of the mere fact of seven hundred and eighty-seven islands all a part of Scotland.

The islands are, with a few important exceptions,

divided into two large groups which are themselves sub-divided into two. The Hebrides to the West consist of an inner and an outer archipelago, while the Northern Isles contain both Orkney and Shetland. There is a difference between the appearance of the Hebrides and Northern Isles. There is an even stronger difference between the characters of those who live upon the main two groups. There is a distinction too between the way of life in the Inner and the Outer Hebrides and between the character of the Orcadian and the Shetlander.

The Western Isles are more famously, more obviously, perhaps it would be fairer to say more immediately beautiful than the northern group. There must be few visitors with an eye for natural scenery who, being fortunate enough to come to the Hebrides in fine weather, are not at once captured by one or another aspect of these infinitely variable islands with their golden and silver sands, their profuse or magnificently sombre colouring, their mountains, blue and yellow and soft in the light of summer, or black, grand, and overpowering as they stand against the storm. They have little reserve in their appeal. And though one may never grow tired of them they seem eager to give themselves away in a thousand different ways at a thousand different times. But, and this is the magical thing about them, they never do give themselves away completely.

The Northern Isles are more reserved. To begin with they are not mountainous, and are seldom even impressively precipitous. Nor are their colours generous. Rather they are subtle, quiet – an infinite variation upon greys and greens that melt into the surrounding sea and sky. They do not impress themselves upon the newcomer but insinuate themselves gradually into his consciousness.

And having become aware of them in this way he will not look for them to change. Nor will he ever forget them. If a man has once fallen under the peculiar allurement of Shetland he will find upon his travels in the bright and variegated South that his mind will return for refreshment again and again to the quiet greys and greens, the long lasting half light and the wide horizons of these scattered pieces of land that lie between the North Atlantic and the North of the North Sea. He will find too that they will return to his memory unbidden unexpectedly and sometimes, yes *sometimes*, even more insistently than do the splendours of the Hebrides. This is their own magical quality.

But if there is a difference between the Hebrides and the Norse Islands there is an even greater disparity in the characters of those who live upon them. There is more difference between them than between the Cornishman and the East Anglian, between the Provençal and the Norman, between the Tyrolese and the Prussian Pomeranian peasant. Not only is the Hebridean different from the Norse islander in race, temperament, blood, behaviour, and often religion, but he has a different language; and his remoter history is one long story of the struggle between his forefathers and the forefathers of the Orcadians and the Shetlanders. Indeed, even the most fervent Scottish patriot, even the strongest supporter of the belief that there is an essential national unity built up by history which overrides all the human differences within the land and islands of Scotland sometimes finds it difficult to reconcile himself to the fact that the Orcadian and the man from Barra in the outer Hebrides are both Scotsmen. But they are.

The Hebrides are the purest repositories of the Celtic

tradition, the Celtic language and the Celtic way of life in all Scotland. And the fact that the blood of the Hebridean, especially in the North-West, has a strong dash of remote Norse mixture introduced by the raiders of centuries ago, only underlines the predominant Celtic quality in these islands. When you see a tall Hebridean whose fair hair, blue eyes, high cheek-bones mark him out from the darker, smaller, more obviously Celtic of his neighbours, you may be sure that he is descended from the Vikings who ravaged, conquered, withdrew from, and then ravaged these islands again, less than a thousand years ago. However, when you hear him talking Gaelic or see in his behaviour, his laughter, his eloquent speech, his some-times even more eloquent silence, those unmistakable traits of the Scottish Gael you will have observed a living example of a conqueror who has been conquered. The Vikings may have ravaged the Celtic Islands with all the ferocity of which they were capable, they may have put the men to the sword, possessed the women, and ruled over the land in their wild and capricious way, but in the long run it was they themselves who were absorbed into the Celtic West and who succumbed, as so many others have done in these islands, to the insidious, gentle, but in the end powerful influence of the Gael whom they conquered.

In the Hebrides the Celtic quality in the inhabitants has survived, despite the presence of modern life and despite the terribly weakening effects of emigration and nineteenth-century landlordism, because there has been nothing else, humanly speaking, to take its place. Nothing that has yet happened to the Western Isles has been able to remove the 'Celtic feel' of them; and that Celtic feel does not spring solely from the beauty of the islands, but from a human factor which has not yet been eliminated from them.

In Shetland and Orkney, however, particularly in Orkney, the Norse strain has survived and in places flourished because of its own independent vigour. The Norse islanders of Scotland are, on the whole, a practical people who make the best of life as they find it. And many of them have certainly and most effectively made the best of their remote northern habitations. Some of them are excellent farmers, amongst the best in Scotland, and others are excellent and practical seamen – easily the best in the country. Some of them are great voyagers who know every great port in both hemispheres, but when they are done with travel they do not, as the Gaels so often do, waste their longing in dreams of home, but, usually and more practically, return to spend a tolerably contented evening of their days in Orkney or Shetland. On the other hand, those who choose to stay and work the land, even when they have become rich and successful, have little desire to spend their substance in seeing the world, but remain in their islands which provide all they want. Up till the outbreak of the 1939 war there were said to be some well-to-do Orkney farmers who possessed expensive motor cars, had often travelled by air between the various islands of their group, but who had never had the curiosity to visit the mainland of Scotland (or just 'Scotland' as they call it) who had consequently never seen a railway train. It is interesting to reflect that these prosperous and often well-educated men had passed clean over the nineteenth century. In their childhood they could remember a time when the horse was the only means of transport; in their latter middle-age they were accustomed to petrol both upon the roads and in the air, but had never known the blessings or the curse of land travel by steam.

The habit, both in Orkney and in Shetland, of calling the largest island in each group 'the mainland' and referring to the main bulk of Scotland as 'Scotland' is characteristic of their innocent and indeed sometimes admirable self-sufficiency. It also arises from an ancient but on the Norse islands an obstinately remembered fact. Orkney and Shetland were the latest islands to become a part of the Scottish kingdom; for it is less than five hundred years ago since they were pledged by the Crown of Norway to the Crown of Scotland in place of a marriage dowry and were never reclaimed. For a long time, when there was still some faint hope of the dowry being paid, the Norse islanders clung to the belief that they were rightfully a part of Norway. Nor did the oppressive treatment which they received at the hands of their Scottish overlords make them feel any love for Scotland. Their remoteness allowed this sense of independence to continue long after there was any question of their return to Norway, that is after the Union of the Crowns of England and Scotland, and subsequently the Union of Parliaments. Indeed, up till half-way through the eighteenth century, and while their 'Old Norse' language still faintly survived, the Shetlander and the Orcadian continued to feel themselves foreigners when they visited the main part of Scotland. This sense of foreignness was more acute than the feeling of being a proud stranger which the Hebridean felt, and still partly feels when he comes to the mainland. The Hebrideans' Gaelic language may have survived more vigorously than Old Norse, but the Gael has always felt from his history that Scotland has belonged to him and not he to Scotland.

When you visit the Norse Isles to-day, particularly Shetland, you cannot fail to notice that something of this feeling of independence from Scotland still exists. Your host will tell you about it within the first day of your arrival, and you will see references to it in the local and flourishing Press. The peasants in the remoter islands as well as the shopkeepers in Lerwick will talk about making a visit to Scotland, will refer to the plane or boat from Scotland, and sometimes will talk about an incomer (but in friendly terms) as a Scotsman. Quite certainly 'The Mainland' will mean nothing to anyone but the largest island of the group. The Orkney and Shetland dialect – again this is stronger in Shetland – contains a number of Norse words which are unfamiliar to the Scottish ear, or can be recognized only with difficulty as having remote relationship to Scots.

This independence of the Norse islander comes, as has been said, from history and from something in the character of the people. At the same time it must be remembered that though Orkney and Shetland have had their persecutions from the South many centuries ago they did not suffer anything like the calculated oppression brought to bear upon the Gael in his islands and in the Highlands of Scotland. Landlordism in the last century had its evils in Shetland and Orkney, but it was never as pernicious as in the Hebrides. Whether the Norse islander would have resisted with greater effect a policy of oppression and expulsion of the kind the Hebridean and the Gaelic Highlander had to endure is something that we cannot now decide. One thing, however, is certain (and it is something that marks most clearly the difference between the two groups of islanders); if the Norse islander had been thrust out and away from the land of his ancestors he might have left as sullenly and as sadly as the exiled Hebridean, but he would have left silently and without a song.

'In a thousand years the Orkneyman has not made a song.' This gibe of the Highlander against his Northern neighbour is not strictly true: it would certainly not be true of the Shetlander. But anyone who has travelled amongst the Scottish islands and has got to know them can understand the force of the remark, especially when it comes from Gaelic lips. The Hebridean can make poetry and a song about anything – love, war, religion, fishing, hunting, the catching or losing of the tide, or even the catching or losing of a bus. The Norse literature of antiquity was concerned almost solely with the practical business of conquest; and when the Norseman ceased to conquer and to apply himself to the equally practical business of tilling the land where he had settled down, and fishing the seas around it, he ceased almost entirely to make up imaginative stories.

This is one of the most obvious of the differences between the Norseman and the Hebridean. The Norseman is practical, the Hebridean is poetic, musical, and highly imaginative. This difference produces its effects. The Norse islander makes the best of things, cultivates his land with industry, and is difficult to budge from it, for he comes from a long line that has been accustomed to fighting. The Hebridean is no less virile, and can fight as well, indeed more fiercely, but is poor in retreat, and, having once been convinced of defeat, accepts it with a poetic melancholy, sinking back into the world of his own imagination. And it is not only defeat at the hands of his fellow men that he accepts in this manner. The weather, the hardness of his soil, the capricious behaviour of the herring, all these sometimes prove too much for him; and if they do he is inclined to accept the bitterness of circumstances with a sigh and possibly a song, and not to fight against it. Every few years the heather and the wild growth in Orkney are pushed up the hill as the cultivated land grows under the industry and the skill of the Orcadian farmer. Every year, somewhere in the Hebrides the wild land eats into the farms and crofts. Nor, alas! can one put this down solely to the fact that the Hebrides are being drained of their inhabitants.

It must be repeated, however, that the Hebridean is not lacking in virility. He too has come of a long line of fighters. It is simply that his kind of virility is not the kind that can combat modern circumstances; nor does he seem well able to adapt his proud fighting spirit to that laborious contest against nature which we call farming. The sword and the word have been his traditional weapons rather than the ploughshare. And now that the sword has been taken away from him and has even as an instrument in modern warfare fallen into desuetude he has grown increasingly to rely upon the word – the word of his imagination. 'In the beginning was the Word.' Those who dislike the Gael and are repelled by his way of life (there are some) would say that it will be in the word that that Hebridean will find his end.

The Hebridean, like all Celts, is highly sensitive to the beauty of this world, but finds solace for the ugliness and the sorrows in it in his belief that the flesh and what the flesh perceives is transitory. He is therefore radically religious, clinging to the old-established faiths, either the stricter and more mystical forms of Presbyterianism or, in certain islands, Catholicism. His sensitiveness to beauty makes him take a keen and sensuous pleasure in the simple things around him, and he has traditionally loved to express this pleasure in the exquisite *minutiae* of his art, whether in song, colouring or carving. He loves bright colours and gay things, and is either very inhibited or not inhibited at all. He likes to make love with ceremony and much words, sometimes finding (to the annoyance of the loved one) satisfaction in the words alone. All this is very different from the Norse islander's way of life. He is without 'such nonsense'; is not temperamentally very religious, does not care much for colours and farms his land and mates with his women with a practical vigour which renders them both fruitful.

These are the main differences between the islander from the two main groups. But, as has been said, there are differences within the groups themselves. This is partticularly true of the Northern Islands where there is a marked distinction between the Shetlander and the Orcadian. This distinction has been expressed in the popular saying that the Orkney man is a farmer who has a boat, and the Shetlander is a fisherman who has a croft.

This sums up neatly the most obvious and outward difference, but there are other distinctions of character. The Orcadian is not only a farmer but a very good farmer. It is a surprising and exhilarating experience for those who think that the island of Great Britain in general, and Scotland in particular, grow progressively more barren the farther north one gets to visit Orkney for the first time in summer. Having passed through scenes of increasing austerity (and beauty) since leaving Edinburgh or Glasgow one crosses that narrow strip of water which connects the Atlantic and the North Sea, the channel so dreaded by those subject to seasickness, the Pentland Firth, and comes to a land of closely gathered rather than scattered islands which, though barren of trees and beaten upon by the winds is obviously rich in the fruits of farming. Small wonder then that the Orcadian whose patient but always progressive industry has made this remote Northern archipelago flourish and multiply in its produce shows the virtues of sound practical commonsense, hard work, and reliability.

It is understandable, too, that he should look with a slight air of superiority upon his fellow Norse islander from Shetland whose efforts with his admittedly more barren land have been much more modest and less successful. What he would think of the Hebridean is difficult to imagine – but then he never does think of him. But the Shetlander, being closer to him in blood and in geography, does come under his cousinly scrutiny; and he is inclined to think of him as a shiftless fellow. In this he exaggerates unjustly. No race that has produced such magnificent seamen both in British waters and on the oceans of the world can really be called shiftless, or be blamed for his wandering eye and mobile imagination. And if the Shetlander is inclined to take life leisurely upon his croft when he gets home and to leave more of the work to his women than the Orcadian would consider dignified, he is only enjoying that reaction from life at sea which is natural to all sailors and particularly to sailors of daring and skill. Nevertheless one cannot deny that the Shetlander's tendency to let things drift on his own homeland has had its evil effects. Orkney is one of the most prosperous parts of Great Britain. Shetland most certainly is not. Though whether the Shetlander is a more agreeable and easy fellow to get along with, a more winning personality than the Orcadian, is another question.

In appearance both groups of islands are obviously
Northern, almost to the extent of looking foreign. The
charming little capital towns of Lerwick in Shetland and
Kirkwall in Orkney with their narrow streets that protect
the citizens from the howling winter winds, and their
paving stones that run right across from house to house,
have a distinctly Scandinavian air. The long summer
days, and the brief grey intervals of light at midwinter
encourage in the visitor a sense of remoteness, as if he had
come to the edge of the world. Orkney with its reddish
soil, its cultivated fields, shows more colour than does
Shetland; but it is in Shetland that the true luminous
beauty of the Northern light is to be seen at its best during the long-drawn-out twilight known to the Shetlanders
by the evocative name of 'the simmer dim'.

Lovely though these midsummer Shetland nights may
be, the most nearly perfect St John's Eve that the present
writer has ever enjoyed in Northern Europe was spent in
Orkney. And it was the colours or rather the behaviour of
the Orcadian colours that provided the magic of that
entrancing midnight. He had, on the 23rd of June, come
in from fishing on a loch on the mainland of Orkney at
about 10 in the evening; for there was a dead calm, and
the unruffled water with its maddening plop of trout all
over the glossy surface offered a chance for the wet fly to
deceive. He beached his boat and went up the hillside to
lie in the heather and await the possibility of a breeze in
the morning. But there was no morning, only the melting
of one day into the next through a limbo of twilight that
seemed neither short nor long but timeless. The effect
which this grey intermediary period that passed for night
produced was unforgettable.

At 10 o'clock the midsummer colours of Orkney were

still bright, even garish, upon the low hillsides. The soil was red, the grass green, the poppies and the pernicious mustard plant scattered amidst the grass were scarlet and a bright yellow, and the sea and the loch a hard blue; for all were catching the last light of the sun. When the short night fell these colours drained out of the scene while one looked at them. The landscape did not lose its shape but merely took on the monochrome of a photograph. Then as the new day began all that happened was that the soil became red again, the grass green, the mustard plant yellow, the poppies scarlet, and the sea and the loch blue. The colours flowed back into the countryside like blood into the face of a happy human being. To the watcher on the hillside that midsummer morning did not come from far away and from over the horizon, but out of the very substance of the scene itself, from the flowers and the grasses and the weeds and the rocks and the sea water and the fresh water which were enriching themselves with their own colours again in the light of a day that had never left them, never died but only grown faint against the Northern sky.

The difference between the appearance of the Inner and the Outer Hebrides is more obvious than that between Orkney and Shetland. The inner group which contains the celebrated Island of Skye and the almost equally large Mull and Islay is like a part of the Western Highlands which has been cut off by the sea. The islands are mostly mountainous, highly coloured in summer and autumn and generally striking in their appearance. It is for this reason, as well as because of their comparative accessibility, that they are what the average visitor to Scotland thinks of when he talks about the Hebrides. Few conscientious tourists in Scotland omit Skye from their journeys; and even though they may not go to any of the other islands they cannot avoid seeing them lying out to sea as they go up the West Coast.

The outer Hebrides, composed of the long strip of islands beginning in the north at Lewis and straggling south-westwards to Barra Head, are remote in fact and, in a way which it is difficult to define, in appearance. They have no impressive mountains or 'noble prospects'; nor do they present a profusion of colours. Instead they are, for the most part, undulating or flat, subtly shaded in yellows, greens, and greys, with the rocks always breaking through the sparse earth. Though not so subfusc as Shetland they have something of the same air of ultimate quiet, and lack of 'showiness'. Yet, for those who really know and love the islands it is in this outer group that the true essence of the Hebridean scene, both natural and human, lies.

As the race is predominantly Celtic in both Inner and Outer Hebrides, and the language and culture Gaelic, there is little difference in traditions or way of life between the two groups. Modern life and the tendencies of the last century have, however, borne much more heavily upon the Inner Islands. The curse of emigration has not fallen more disastrously on any part of Scotland than in some of the more immediate and celebrated islands off her Western coast. There are parts of Skye where the population has been reduced to a quarter of its size within the last fifty years. And there are smaller islands where the pathetic prospect of a school with three or four children attending it, and with only a handful of elderly adults dreaming away the evening of their lives, would justify one describing these places as being all but abandoned.

This is the greatest evil affecting the indigenously Celtic parts of Scotland. It has been mentioned at greater length in the chapter dealing with the Highlands. There is little that one can add to the melancholy discussion of the subject as it applies in the islands save to say that it is in places more acute than on the mainland, and that in the Inner Hebrides, where such possible palliatives as the employment of the natives under the Hydro-Electric scheme does not seem immediately practicable, it is even more difficult to think of any solution. But perhaps this reflection may also be added. The scenes of desolation in the smaller islands may not be as overpowering as in the large ravaged areas of the mainland, so impressively disastrous, but the effect upon the observer to-day is more poignant, more pathetic, more heartbreaking.

To describe conditions in the Outer Islands as being more cheerful might seem a condescending way of talk to some of their inhabitants who, too, have had their own bitter and often unsuccessful struggles against modern conditions and nineteenth-century evictions. It might indeed seem near insulting to a crofter in Uist who can see at his doorstep the immediate evidences of a policy of desolation which had begun long before he was born, and which had become so nearly complete as to be discontinued in his lifetime. Nevertheless the mere remoteness as well as the apparent barrenness and the lack of the scenic splendour to be found in the Inner Hebrides has protected 'the Long Island', which is the Highland name for the whole length from Lewis to Barra, in the past from the depredations of rich sportsmen and profiteering landlords. This remoteness, too, has encouraged in the Gael of the Outer Islands a stronger tenacity in holding on to his way of life, his religion, and his language. This is as true of the fairly populous and comparatively modern and rigidly Presbyterian town of Stornoway in Lewis as it is of the more scattered rural and Roman Catholic inhabitants of Barra. Any visitor from the mainland of Scotland who has the leisure to travel in both groups of the Hebrides cannot, whether he approve of it or not, but be struck by the greater degree of Gaelic self-sufficiency in 'the Long Island'.

At the time of writing these words the largest island of the Outer Hebrides and its capital of 5000 inhabitants, Stornoway, is suffering one of its periodic and what looks like one of its severest bouts of economic depression. This depression is infecting nearly all the islands to south of it, that is to say those whose trade has for nearly a century depended upon the making of tweed. The most celebrated of these islands is, of course, Harris. It is a depression which has been acute enough to cause alarm on the mainland and to call for Parliamentary investigation. But two things should be remembered. These periods of depression are not new in the islands; and this one has been brought about by outside means, by the ineptitude of trying to apply laws about the manufacture of tweed suitable for Bradford to the Outer Islands. It is not an evil which has arisen within the island itself, but one which can be cured by outside action if it is quickly taken.

There are other depressing factors present in the state of all the Long Island. And it would be folly beyond the most fatuous optimism of the most professionally optimistic politician to pretend that things are not, as they have been for a long time, bad in the Outer Islands and that that badness is approaching a chronic state. At the same time it would be, for those who feel for the Gaelic way of life, the dreariest form of determinism to accept the view that this evil is endemic, incurable, and will result in the death of the Gael in the Outer Hebrides, or his complete and inevitable expulsion from them. No, the wonder is not that the Gael has suffered so grievously here and has shown signs as a race of his suffering, but that he should have survived so well and should have kept his culture so comparatively intact.

Stornoway is a town by rural standards of some size: it is also a Gaelic town; and is becoming more Gaelic in speech and custom every year. Stornoway may have been colonized by the fishermen of Fife many years ago, as this part of the Outer Isles was ravaged and semi-colonized by the Norsemen centuries earlier, but the same process is operating in the descendants of the East of Scotland in-comers as operated on the Vikings. The influence of the Gael is predominating. It is coming out of something in the soil, in the air of the place preserved by generations of Celts. And it is a natural and not a consciously imposed or induced process. Indeed for all its mixture of blood there is a strong case to be made out for Stornoway being a town where the natural spring of Gaelic and the Celtic way of life is stronger, more quietly persistent than it is in any town of a like size you care to mention in the consciously Gaelic State of the Irish Republic.

If this be true of the modern and racially mixed Stornoway at the north end of the Long Island, how much more so is it true of the islands that straggle out south and west of the largest and main island of Lewis where the blood is not mixed, or if it be mixed is of so ancient a mixture that the Gael has triumphed in his own inevitable fashion. And how clearly, too, can that truth be recognized not as a mere vague impression but as a fact at the

extreme south-west tip in the Barra islands, with which
it is only fair to include the celebrated Eriskay of the
'love lilt'.

It is easy for the Celtic enthusiast to sentimentalize over
Barra and the Barra islands. It is equally easy for the professional denigrator of the Highland and Celtic way of
life whose theme is the continual repetition of the statement that the day of the native and remaining Celt is
over, that he is finished, to seize upon the evidences of this
sentimentality as an excuse for dismissing the strong fact
of the Barra islander's way of life as a mere fantasy. It is
easy for him to say that in his ultimate stronghold of a
Scotland that has been forgotten elsewhere there is nothing but an anachronism which has survived by accident
to be treasured by 'escapists' and romantics, nothing but a
remote people who have remotely preserved a few lovely
songs which can be made musically comprehensible if
they are not nasally 'keened' in the native fashion but are
subject to the refining process of being sung by a trained
metropolitan voice and set to the accompaniment of the
pianoforte. The fact remains, however, that in the Barra
islands you have not only a survival of the old Celtic
Scotland, but as compared with anywhere else in the
country a vigorous survival. In Barra itself, an island
which you can walk round in a day, there is a population
of nearly three thousand. Most of the men are crofters,
amongst whom the land is divided, or fishermen who own
or have combined to own their boats. This state of independence has not been achieved without a painful
struggle, which reached its climax and victory just before
the first World War. It is true that in the process of that
struggle the population declined, but that decline was as
nothing compared with the obliteration of whole com-

unities in other parts of the Highlands and Islands. It true also that despite the victory in their struggle for dependence the Barra islanders have had to face and ill do contend with many difficulties arising from their moteness. And it would indeed be offensively and patronizingly sentimental for the visitor who falls under the harm of the island and its inhabitants to suppose that ey lead an idyllic existence upon the edge of the world, ie world forgetting, by the world forgot. But it is no less bsurd and unjust to pass over the fact, as some people o, that these remote representatives of a race so often boken of as dying beyond hope have in these Atlantic lands struggled and fought for independence, have chieved it, relish their victory and are happy in it.

For that the Gael on Barra is happy, happy in the way nat men are who are not thwarted and who are fulfilling hemselves, is obvious to anyone who knows the island, ven to those who come to it for a short visit. He has naturally, and to the full, the Celtic contempt for time vhich seems to the Saxon a kind of fecklessness. But this ias not eaten into his native vigour nor destroyed his purpose. He can be indolent too when he wants to be, but only when he feels inclined. His is not the sad laziness of o many proud Highlanders who have surrendered to the Highland history and seem to have had indolence imposed upon them. The Barra man has fought for his victory too hard for that to happen to him. Moreover, he has to work too hard in order to keep the fruits of his victory. The people of Barra are emotional and uninhibited, and are, on the whole, humorous and gay in demeanour, without that haunting melancholy which afflicts so many of their race elsewhere in Scotland. They are musical and poetic; and it is from their islands that have come many

of those 'Songs of the Hebrides' whose peculiar magic h
enabled them to survive the process of being refined ar
adapted to concert hall taste. One of the purest Nativi
songs in the whole of Christendom is 'The Chri
Child's Lullaby' from Eriskay.

The mention of this island hymn raises one of the mo
important facts about the people of Barra; and that
that with the exception of a small number of incomers tl
population is fervently but quite simply Catholic. As h;
been said earlier in this chapter the Hebrideans are t
nature deeply religious and cling to the traditional forn
of Christianity. In the Northern Hebrides and on near
all the inner group this religious conservatism express
itself in a rigid form of Presbyterianism which has large
lost its grip elsewhere in Scotland. There are those wh
laugh at the Lewisman's obstinate retention of his 'We
Free' faith and others who are irritated by it. To som
however, this uncompromising affirmation of his creed
not without its admirable qualities. In the Barra islanc
the people have clung to a faith with a longer traditior
and yet one which in our modern world remains mor
alive. They have clung to it over the centuries despit
bitter persecution in the past. They now have their re
ward. For it is a singular fact that this persecution has le
no mark on these islands of free uninhibited people. The
take their Catholic Faith there simply without questior
and without the bitterness of controversy. At times i
seems as if they have passed over the Reformation un
touched. The Barra islands may remain the purest repo
sitory of the old Celtic Scotland that is left, but it is a
repository in which that old Scotland still lives as well a
remains; and it is linked, as was the old Scotland, with
the central Faith of Europe. He who attends the Mass o

the Day on Sundays and Holy Days in Barra will hear the Epistle and the Gospel sung or spoken in the same words as those used in St. Peter's, Rome, that same morning. He will hear also that Epistle and Gospel read from the pulpit in a language 'understanded of the people', a language which is older even than Latin. And as he hears the Latin and the Gaelic he will know that though he is upon a remote island in the Atlantic he is not severed from the heart of Christendom.

Is it out of proportion to have devoted so large a part of this book to the seven hundred and eighty-seven islands of Scotland which, despite their number, contain only a small minority of the number of people who live in the country? And does it appear in what he has written that the author has exercised a private predilection in attaching such importance to a community inhabiting one of the furthest and, by some, the most forgotten of these islands? Perhaps; but, if an excuse be needed, it is this: No one can fully understand the complex character of the Scottish people unless he takes into account the influence which these many and diverse islands have had upon it – these islands which Scotland has thrown out from the body of herself to the North and the West of her mainland, islands from which she continues to draw the continual refreshment of her own essence. And above all, no one should accept without question the often repeated statement that the Gaelic way of life in Scotland is dying, doomed or dead without pausing to consider the existence, the fact of Barra.

CHAPTER EIGHT

RELIGION

AFTER the birth of the nation and the establishment of its survival by the will of the people and by force of arms the most important event in the life of Scotland has been the Reformation. This was true four hundred years ago; it is as true to-day. Not Flodden field, not the Union of the Crowns, not even the loss of her Parliament nor the Industrial Revolution so profoundly affected and continue to affect every person in the country from the remotest island in the North Atlantic to the flats of Wigtown – with Ireland across the narrow seas or to the English border where the Anglican bishoprics and the rule of English law end.

This great and sombre event, glorious or destructive according to your faith or your reading of history (for it incontestably showed forth the glory of heroism and the rage of destruction), touches every one of us in Scotland. It has affected the structure of our whole society and the way we think and act. Even the remote Catholic Highlander or Hebridean, however much in harmony he may live with his Protestant neighbour, cannot but be influenced by the fact that his community forms an ancient but isolated minority in a long-established majority which has struck deep roots. Even the town-dwelling atheist or agnostic or the man apparently and, in his own view, comfortably indifferent to religion living in Glasgow, Edinburgh, Dundee, or Aberdeen cannot even in the smallest way play his part in the life around him without feeling the effect of this event that happened so long ago. Outwardly it will regulate the forms of much of the way in which he passes his daily life, and will control or at least influence his leisure and relaxation in public.

Inwardly, though he may be unconscious of this or even deny it, it is likely to have left its impress on his philosophy, if he has one, and on his behaviour and his attitude towards the outside world. The Protestant Reformation of the Christian faith in the Scottish form of that Reformation has contributed to the making of his mind in its deepest places. And how true this is both for himself and his companions! However earnestly he may reject the tenets of the Christian Faith in general, however indignantly he may repel the need for reformation within himself, the average modern Scot who is neither Roman Catholic nor Episcopalian remains a product of the Scottish Reformed Christian Kirk.

The Reformation, as has been said in an earlier chapter, is the great watershed that divides the millennium of Scotland's story. It is a watershed from which a large number of the burns and rivers that flow down into our present life in Scotland proceed. We cannot, however much we keep our feet out of them, escape the influences of them on and underneath the land we tread. They seep through and touch us upon the soles of our feet, and as cold water touching a man's feet will chill or invigorate his whole body so the Scottish Reformation has chilled or invigorated, even inflamed, the whole of Scotland since it was made by us. For our Reformation was, though it may not have been conceived by us, made by us, fashioned after our own ideas.

This watershed of the Reformation is so obvious, it so overshadows nearly all the last half of Scotland's story since she became a nation, that there is a popular tendency, sometimes encouraged in the cruder text books, to think of Scotland as really only beginning to be herself when she expelled the priests and shook herself free of the spiritual authority of Rome. This is, of course, a gross error. For while it is true that modern Scotland began with John Knox, the Scottish nation had been founded five hundred years before Knox was born, and had been taking on the shape of its character vigorously throughout that half millennium. This error is as absurd as a man of fifty saying that he had only begun to exist after he was thirty and rejecting all influences on himself before that date. Naturally no Scottish Catholic would take this point of view about his country's past; no modern Protestant or Presbyterian scholar would hold it either; and most thinking Scotsmen who have any sense of history would agree with them. They would agree that you cannot begin to comprehend Scotland until you look at her whole story – both before and after the Reformation.

Amongst Scotsmen of a religious cast of mind who are not Catholic or sympathetic to the Catholicism there are two attitudes to the pre-Reformation Church in Scotland which prevail. The old-fashioned point of view, which is a legacy from the days of the Reformation itself and later from the struggle against Protestant Episcopacy, is that all Catholic Scotland was in matters of religion given over to error and to evil. The other point of view which has been gaining favour in modern Presbyterian circles is that the Scottish pre-Reformation Church was founded in the Celtic rather than in the Latin tradition of Christianity, that only in the end and before the Reformation did it become corrupted by Romanism and that the traditions of the old Celtic form are still alive in Presbyterianism to-day and can be fostered in a truly national church. Those who hold the first view are suspicious of the latter and more modern group, fearing that in their casting back to the 'traditions of St Columba' they may be opening the door to Romish influences or, in some mysterious way which is never defined, Anglicizing Scotland's national kirk. On the other hand, the 'St Columbans' within the Church of Scotland are impatient of what seems to them a narrow and an unhistorical view of Scottish Christianity.

The more old-fashioned and implacable point of view is on the decline. Less and less are religious Scotsmen ready to dismiss over twenty generations of their Christian forebears in Scotland as being given over in matters of religions entirely to error and evil, and, while not for a moment questioning the need for reform in the past, more and more of them would take a tolerant view of that past. In certain places, however, this rock-like tradition of Scottish Protestantism lives on – in the remoter Highlands, in certain country places, and in groups in the larger towns, though these last have sometimes political as well as religious origins. The tradition survives too in some Scots who would not describe themselves as practising Christians, Presbyterian or otherwise, or who may indeed be actively opposed to religion. Regarding all dogmatic and formal Christianity as superstitious they naturally look upon the Catholic period of their country's history as being the era of the blackest superstition in that kind. But in many of these there is a deeper feeling than reason which makes them repel the religion and even more strongly the ritual of Rome: it is a feeling which they have acquired in their blood from past generations who have succeeded in transmitting to their posterity their religious antagonisms but not their religious faith.

The other attitude, that of the 'St Columban' Presbyterians to pre-Reformation Scotland, is, of course, a more modern, a nineteenth-century conception and has not entered into the feeling of the people as did the spirit of the seventeenth-century reformers. But while it has certain historical justifications it too can be and is exaggerated. It is true that the northern Church that began with St Ninian and St Columba, and traced an unbroken descent from the year 397 A.D., drew in its origins from the Eastern as well as from the Western traditions. It is true that in some respects it resembled the Uniate Churches of the East at the present day which, although in Communion with Rome, preserve their own liturgies and customs. It is true also that in the long quarrel over the date of Easter that was conducted between the Celtic Churchmen and their Southern brethren the Celts displayed an intransigence that reminds one of certain elements in modern Scotland. So great was this intransigence that it provoked from Cumnian ironic words which have a familiar ring down the centuries: 'Rome is in error, Jerusalem is in error, Antioch is in error. The whole world is in error. Only the Britons' (the inhabitants of South-West Scotland) 'and the Scots possess the truth'. Everyone, in short, was 'oot o' step except oor Jock'.

All this is true. But the more one examines the celebrated and now much spoken of independence of the early Celtic Church one perceives that what our clerical predecessors were fighting against was not so much Central European and Latin authority but the channels through which that authority was supposed to reach them

from the Saxon lands. And even with the guardians of
these channels they were prepared to come to terms when
it was proper to do so. It should not be forgotten that at
the Synod of Whitby in 664 the Northern Church, with a
large spirit of generosity, with a practical sense of the
good of Western Christianity and of the Universal
Church, entered into an agreement with this same Southern and Saxon Church. Those who claim that unreason-
able intransigence, 'oor Jockism', is endemic in the Scot,
and is profoundly radical in his history, should pause to
consider this event in our distant past which remains one
of the most celebrated examples of 'toeing the line' for
the general good in the whole history of the Christian
Church.

It would be tedious to support the example of the
large and undeniable facts of the Synod of Whitby with
other proofs of the equally undeniable fact that members
of the early Celtic Church considered themselves to be a
part of the Universal Church in communion with Rome
and a part of Western Christendom. But it would be
equally vain to deny the individualities in liturgy and
custom of that early Celtic Church.

Finally, it would be impossible here to enter into the
highly controversial discussion of the reforms in liturgy,
customs, and moral theology as well which Margaret,
Saint and Queen, instituted in the Scottish Church during the reign of her husband King Malcolm Canmore.
Even to mention the name of that truly saintly and truly
remarkable woman nearly nine hundred years after her
death and almost exactly seven hundred years after her
reception into Paradise is enough to bring a storm of
Gaelic dispute about one's ears. It is sufficient to state the
incontrovertible fact that through these reforms the

Scottish Church at the end of the eleventh century was brought into complete and outward conformity with the Western and Latin Church, with which she had always been in communion. For near upon five hundred years this conformity was to remain. Not only did it remain, it flourished and produced its effects. Scotland during this half millennium was, to use a modern expression, much more Continental-minded than her Southern neighbour. This, combined with the now established religious conformity, made her, in the words of Mr Walter Elliot in a remarkable essay published in *The Times Literary Supplement* under the title of 'Jesus and No Quarter,' 'a microcosm of Europe, in a sense the great fenced, fertile, self-centred, metropolitan country of England to the South never was'.

All this admitted, indeed proclaimed, there would be no point in denying the earlier individualities in liturgy and custom in the Scottish Church, or the lingering effects of them. To quote Mr Elliot again: 'Christianity in Scotland, Ninianic and Columban, drew in its beginnings both on the Eastern and on the Western tradition, nor did either of the two strands ever disappear (the monks of Iona were obtaining their pigments from Mount Athos as late as the thirteenth century), and when the storm broke many old reefs started spouting seawards.' 'The storm', in this context, is, of course, the Reformation.

The most remarkable feature of that remarkable postwar enterprise, the annual Festival of the Arts in Edinburgh, has been the repeated productions of Sir David Lindsay's *Ane Satire of the Thrie Estaitis*. In its form this four-hundred-year-old morality play is a kind of Scottish *Everyman*, but its theme, as its title proclaims, is satire. It is a bitter, witty, pungent, and passionate comment in the

Scots language of the sixteenth century on the misgovernment of the realm by the clergy, the nobles, and the merchants, and their enslavement of the personality of the young king whose luxury, sensuality, and indolence have softened his fundamental nobility of character, and made him an easy, but as it turns out only temporary, prey of these decadent and vicious three estates of the Realm. There can be no doubt that it was intended as a dramatic and contemporary picture of the state of affairs in Scotland during the reign of James V, the last Catholic King, though not the last Catholic monarch to reign in Scotland. Its author, feeling, as he obviously did, the passionate urgency of his theme, and luxuriating in the Renaissance manner in the richness of his language, may have exaggerated in his highly dramatic treatment of the venality, villainy, and luxury of the clergy in the Three Estates. Maybe, but that does not detract from the obvious sincerity of the writing, nor does it affect one of the most interesting facts about the play.

Most of the visitors from abroad and many of the native Scots who have thronged each year to see *The Thrie Estaitis* must have supposed that this was a characteristically Scottish product of the early Scottish Reformation at its most vigorous and in its most outspoken mood. Indeed one critic compared it to Knox's tremendous denunciations. They would, however, have been wrong. Lindsay was a practising Roman Catholic who, as far as we know, died in the Faith in which he was born and had certainly not abjured it at the time of the writing and first production of the play. Even more interesting is the fact that this huge piece (in its original form it lasted nine hours) was played before the Court of James V at Linlithgow to the enjoyment of a large crowd, and that its Edinburgh performance was said to be at the command of that ardent Catholic, Mary of Lorraine.

The statement of these facts is a simple way of putting before the reader a truth which, though it can be and often is treated controversially, is not denied by any responsible Catholic historian. And that is that the Church in Scotland immediately before the Reformation was riddled with abuses and was corrupt in high places. These facts also show that these abuses were a public matter and gave deep concern to contemporary Catholics as well as providing fuel in the popular mind for the Protestant Reformation that was to come.

When that Reformation was by law established in Scotland at the Parliament of Edinburgh in 1560 most of the powerful men who brought it into being were actuated by political motives, which need not concern us here. Their actions, however, were made easier by the people's memory of these abuses in the Church during the preceding century, and by the example of the heroism of the humbler Protestant martyrs who had died resisting a Church which had contained these abuses. It would be a mistake, however, to suppose that the powerful nobles and men of State who fought over the early Reformation in Scotland on either side were concerned much with morals or were deeply disturbed on matters of faith. Their struggles were political; but out of that struggle they unleashed, almost without being aware of it, beneath, around, and eventually above them a tremendous national conviction and convulsion which was to seize the country.

When that convulsion rose from beneath and around these scheming nobles and men of State of either persuasion and ascended to the throne it discovered in the persons of Mary Queen of Scots and John Knox two contestants worthy of its true quality. They lifted it above the sordid material squabbles of power-hungry men and gave it greatness. Mary and Knox in their persons also gave the highest attributes of drama to their deathless dispute. But the ultimate greatness of that dispute lay in something more than the dramatic qualities described by Mr Elliot in the essay already quoted:

Out of the quarrelsome wynds of Edinburgh, trained in the unlikely surroundings of a tutor of small boys, came suddenly, in middle age, a scholar, an orator, a philosopher, a skilled and crafty politician, a citizen of Europe, a companion to Calvin and, according to his lights, a minister of God. Out of the Court of the French Renaissance, trained and instructed by Mary of Guise, came, in her first youth and beauty, the Queen of Scotland and of France, passing like a comet through the sky of the North, to lead in dances, to lead in battles, to bring herself to the edge of death by a long and perilous ride over hill tracks and morasses to see her wounded lover, to hold her own in logomachy with the most formidable controversialist of her nation, to die, still young, at the order of her hostess, also a woman, also a Queen — and to leave a son who should inherit both their thrones.

This is well said. But there was something more which gave the meeting of two such persons in such circumstances its true greatness. Mary may have been the kind of woman with whom men will fall in love so long as history is written and read *parce qu'elle était plus femme que les autres*; Knox may have been the ultimate expression of harsh unyielding masculinity; both may have been influenced by political motives; both may have been such sinners that in modern eyes they may seem hardly to have been a suitable pair to have been the leaders of two religious parties in a State enduring the agonies and ecstasies of a religious transition; indeed, many questions which we consider to-day to be moral or morally a part of religion may have been quite irrelevant to their passionate religious logomachy. But there was something more, something that transcended all this, something beside which their politics, their political manoeuvrings, their loves, their hates, and even their sins were small matters. It was the cause of their dispute, the greatest cause of all — man's immortal soul.

This these two knew in their time. And this also generations of their compatriots who have lived and died since, who are alive now, have known and still know. It is for this reason, rather than because of the high drama of their living and contending, that the names of Mary and Knox survive most potently in Scotland; for this is a country in which men have an ineradicable preoccupation with their immortal souls, and where logical argument presents to them 'the same almost fleshly satisfaction as it does to the French'.

The argument between the Queen and the Calvinist never reached an end. Nor would it have done so had they lived and argued through the centuries while the walls of Holyrood crumbled about their ears. 'In my end is my beginning' was Mary's motto. In the end her argument would have been where it began, an assertion of Faith. And so also it would have been with Knox whose Faith was no less rock-like, but who had greater strength. In the finish of matters it was that strength which decided the practical outcome; the Queen lost and Knox triumphed. Mary in a few years was a fugitive from her country and nineteen years later was put to death by Elizabeth, her cousin and Queen of England. In the meantime the tremendous personality of Knox had achieved the Reformation in Scotland of which he was the architect. No Scotsman since his day has had, for good or for ill, so large an effect upon his country.

In the seventeenth century Scotsmen of the Reformed Faith struggled not against Rome, whose power in a material sense was now withdrawn from the whole island of Britain, but against the principle of Episcopacy which their own Stuart Kings now on the throne of the United Kingdom sought to impose on them from London. It was this century then which produced that celebrated type of Scottish religious enthusiast who has been held up to the admiration, the detestation, and the mockery of succeeding generations.

All three points of view are comprehensible. No Scotsman of whatever Faith can without a patriotic emotion look back upon the obdurate bigoted heroic Covenanters meeting, at their conventicles upon the hillsides, death with such characteristic fortitude at the hands of the King's Dragoons, whose business it was to shoot down Scots men and women choosing to worship in their own way. No one of us who, upon the now deserted hillsides, comes across the pathetic reminders of those dour heroes, the 'graves of the Martyrs' so poignantly mentioned in Stevenson's poem, can view them without pride as well as sadness. And however ridiculous and sinister (a strange blend that can sometimes occur) the Scottish proposals to change the religion of England by force in the middle of the seventeenth century may seem to us to-day, one cannot withhold admiration for the fanatical bravery of our preposterous zealots. They actually invaded the southern kingdom twice with this end in view and against so formidable a foe as Oliver Cromwell, who paid tribute to them after the battle of Worcester – 'As stiff a contest as I have ever seen'.

No one of a humane cast of mind can now look back without a shiver of distaste amounting to detestation upon the fanatical and cruel dictatorship of the Kirk in the same century, a dictatorship so graphically described in *Witchwood*, a novel by a recent High Commissioner to the General Assembly of the Church of Scotland, and himself a Minister's son – John Buchan. Nor are our attempts to comprehend this almost incredible period in our country's history made any easier by the fact that the world has in recent years suffered from even more ruthless dictatorships, with considerably less spiritual justification.

Finally, since these men are so remote, it is not difficult to see the ludicrous as well as the frightening and admirable qualities they possessed. These ludicrous qualities – the canting, the grotesque excess of Puritanism combined with inevitable hypocrisy – have provided material for much satirical writing. But it took Sir Walter Scott, who understood his own countrymen better than anyone has ever done, to portray in his *Heart of Midlothian* and *Old Mortality* figures that can arouse in us all three feelings, admiration, distaste, and laughter – but with admiration always to the fore.

It was in the seventeenth century also that there began to discover itself in the Reformed religion of Scotland that inescapable Scottish tendency, disunity. At the end of the struggle with Episcopacy and at the founding of the Established Kirk of Scotland the Cameronians ' hived off'. These Cameronians viewed with horror a State Established Church as being an alliance with the powers of darkness. But it was characteristic of their race and kind that the Cameronians did not admit that it was they who had hived off. Rather it was their small body that remained the true Church, and it was the vast majority of their fellow countrymen who had departed from them and the truth. From this time 'hiving off' set in with a vengeance in Reformed religious circles in Scotland. Not only were there fresh seceders from the main body, but there were 'hivers off' from those who had already hived. By the end of the eighteenth century and at the beginning of the nineteenth it was estimated that there were nearly twenty different sects, most of them differing only in small points of doctrine or discipline, but all having originated at various removes from the Presbyterian Church in Scotland as founded at the Reformation.

It is easy to smile at these perhaps over selfconscious expressions of Scottish religious individuality; and it is temptingly easy for the more traditionally-minded to point out that 'this is the sort of thing that is bound to happen as soon as Scotsmen abandon a central authority'. At the same time, now that for practical purposes nearly all these minor branches of Presbyterianism have sunk their differences and joined with the main body, one cannot help feeling that something has been lost in the enthusiasm of Scottish religious life. One cannot help wondering whether this coagulation of sects has really arisen from a genuine desire for a United Protestant Christian front, or whether it has come about owing to creeping indifference and a decline in Faith and numbers. It need hardly be added that there are many who would heartily deny such an assumption.

But the Cameronians or 'Reformed Presbyterians' still survive. There are six congregations in Scotland. The largest church is in their place of origin, the foothills of the Pentland Hills near Edinburgh. This is indeed holy ground for them; for it is near here that their founders suffered martyrdom in the days of the seventeenth-century persecutions. It is impossible not to be touched to admiration by their persistence into this century and time. They still believe that the entire Church of Scotland has hived off from their minute body. They still pray for its return to them and to the light, which they alone contain and perceive. Long may they perceive it.

The present writer was introduced in the way of business to a Cameronian who continued to inhabit out of fidelity this part of Scotland, and who was, a short time ago, verging upon his hundredth year. After their business had been finished the following dialogue took place:

CENTENARIAN CAMERONIAN: And now, sir, I must ask you, are you a religious man?

PRESENT WRITER (*shouting in order to be heard*): I sincerely hope so, sir.

C. C. (*to his grandson*): Is he in a state of grace?

P. W. (*after a pause and seeing that he is expected to reply*): With God's help I hope I am.

C. C. (*after an even longer pause, and as a dreadful doubt dawns upon him*): But maybe you are of ' the Establishment '?

P. W. (*in embarrassment; for he is an adherent of a Church older even than 'the Establishment', but he would hesitate out of tenderness to admit it in these circumstances*): No.

C. C. (*stretching out his hands which have grown so pallid and bloodless with age that they have become all but translucent, and clutching with astonishing strength his interlocutor to his bosom*): So young, so young and, and one of us. ...

The present writer is a man in his middle middle-age, and it seemed to him that this cry of welcome 'So young, so young' from this aged member of a dying but honourable sect was deeply pathetic. He did not comment upon this afterwards, however, but contented himself with asking the old man's grandson what would have happened if he had had to admit the fact that he was a Roman Catholic. 'He wouldn't have minded', was the unexpected reply; 'that's not so bad as "the Establishment".' The seventeenth century was alive again.

At the same time that this hiving off of true religious enthusiasts was going on there were in the eighteenth century Church in Scotland two tendencies. On the one hand, the old Theocracy in its dictator form survived in country places so that even a man so full of independence as Robert Burns was condemned to do penance (and did it) for his sins in public. On the other, there was arising in Edinburgh and the more cultivated and English-influenced circles a school of Scottish Churchmen known as 'the Moderates'. These in part corresponded to the modern 'Broad Church' Anglican school (for by their association with the Edinburgh 'Atheists' the Scottish Churchmen of that time were more 'advanced' in the science of disbelief than were the Anglican clergy) and in part to the easy English State-Church conception of the time. This eighteenth-century Moderatism was repugnant not only to the spirit of the Reformation, but to the Scottish genius which has always abhorred the moderation of compromise.

Such a state of affairs could not last, even in the increasingly refined Scotland of the late eighteenth and early nineteenth centuries. And in 1840 the true and idealistic Scotland discovered itself again in the Disruption of the Church. At this Disruption nearly a third of the Ministers seceded from the State Church, at that time given over to 'moderation and the evils of patronage', and in so doing surrendered, each one of them, not only their manses and their benefices, but their whole livelihoods. It was a noble and a truly national gesture which was rewarded not only in the spiritual satisfaction of those who sacrificed all for a principle but in the support which they received from the country as a whole.

In the late part of last century these seceders joined with the ' United Presbyterians ', another secession body, to form the United Free Kirk. A small remnant refused to join in the union, and they produced that body still powerful in certain parts of the remoter Highlands, commonly known as the ' Wee Frees'. Finally, in 1929 (the points at issue which had brought about the Disruption of 1840 having been settled to everyone's satisfaction) the United Free Kirk reunited with the Established Church. Thus there is once more presented to the world a unified Presbyterian Church of Scotland.

Scotland would not have been Scotland if, in this long process of struggle, disagreement and final near unity there had not been left on the road a variety of dissentients, each one of which had objected to one particular step on the journey and had claimed the immemorial Scottish right to 'hive off', amongst which dissentients incidentally may be numbered our gallant old acquaintances, the Cameronians.

Tempting though it may be for a Scottish author (no matter how much he may be personally detached from these disputes) to expatiate upon the subtleties, the niceties, the rights and wrongs of each one of these separate 'hivings off', he must refrain. One may expect the outside world to note with an aloof interest that we have a national pastime called 'hiving off', and have built up the most complicated conventions and set of rules in connexion with it, but it would be too much to expect the world to be concerned with these *minutiae*.

How then does the Church of Scotland in particular and the Christian Religion in general fare to-day in the Scotland of four hundred years after the Reformation, nine hundred after St Margaret, sixteen hundred after the introduction of Christianity into the country?

In temporal matters it would be fair to say that the Church of Scotland, which has now been reunited with the Free Churches for nearly a quarter of a century, and is thereby strengthened, has held its position and retained the respect of the country. This is partly due to the increasingly independent stand it has taken in certain social and political issues, and partly to the fact of the annual General Assembly. This is a meeting of all the ministers of the Church and certain appointed elders which takes place every spring in Edinburgh. At it matters not only of Church government and principle are discussed, but also those of general Scottish interest. This Assembly derives from the early days of the Reformation, and a representative of the Crown, the High Commissioner, attends. It has been said that Scotland emerged from the Union with England with her key institutions, the Church and the legal system, intact. With the present state of national feeling in Scotland (where two million voters have signed a National Covenant demanding a Scottish Parliament) men are becoming increasingly aware of the value of these key institutions; and whether they be members of the Church of Scotland or not, they are glad of the existence of an Assembly which is the nearest thing to a Parliament that we have left to us. Again, whether Presbyterians or not they feel indignant when resolutions passed by the Assembly, which clearly reflect a large body of Scottish opinion, are politely (and sometimes not even politely) ignored by Westminster. The Church of Scotland may remain an intact key, but its value is reduced if the keyhole four hundred miles South be bunged up with rubbish.

Apart from such purely temporal concerns the Presbyterian Church of Scotland continues to provide for the religiously inclined Scot a philosophy of religious observance and rule to which he is well suited by custom and inclination. This is how a distinguished Presbyterian Divine, Principal Rainy, concludes an eloquent lecture in which he answered Dean Stanley, who had delivered, from the Anglican position, a rather condescending series of lectures on 'The Church of Scotland':

Yes, Presbyterianism is a system for a free people that love a regulated, a self-regulating freedom; for a people independent, yet patient, considerate, trusting much to the processes of discussion and consultation, and more to the promised aid of a much-forgiving and a watchful Lord. It is a system for strong Churches – Churches that are not afraid to let their matters see the light of day – to let their weakest parts and their worst defects be canvassed before men all that they may be mended.

That is how many members of the Church of Scotland would still speak of their Presbyterian religion. And, matters of ultimate Faith in ultimate things apart, it is because they see it in this clear and refreshing light that they would claim that it is particularly suitable for them and their compatriots.

In purely spiritual matters, in its Evangelism to the people of Scotland half way through the twentieth century, it cannot be said that the Church of Scotland has retained its old position. Despite the almost united front it now presents since the Union of 1929 Churches are, Sunday by Sunday, less attended. More and more people, (especially in the towns), who were born and brought up in the Presbyterian Faith, have drifted away from regular observance and have abandoned, for the sake of their convenience, such discipline as the Church had imposed upon them in their childhood and youth. This is particularly noticeable in the decline in the keeping of the Sabbath, once a central point of both faith and discipline in Scottish religious life. Nowhere is the weakening of ministerial, of religious authority in the Presbyterian Church in Scotland more obvious than in this. Sunday after Sunday the early morning streets of our towns are crowded with young men and girls on bicycles or on foot pouring out to spend the day in the country – some of the latter being dressed in costumes which would have appalled most practising Presbyterians even on a week-day forty years ago. And if this early morning efflux is followed later in the day by a more middle-aged exodus in motor cars and buses it is doubtful if more than a minute proportion of those who make it up have spent a part of the morning going to the Kirk.

It must in justice be added that very seldom does one hear from these young and middle-aged Sabbath breakers who snatch at their one whole free day of the week to enjoy the Scottish countryside the excuse that they 'prefer to worship God underneath the blue dome of Heaven and on the hillside rather than in a stuffy church'. Shades of Knox and Mary! This particular form of cant, whose adherents have been so well described by a late Anglican Archbishop as 'the Blue Domers' has not penetrated much North of the Border.

It cannot be denied that this large rejection of the observance of the Sunday is only one of the most obvious signs of a decline of spiritual authority in the Church of

Scotland. Whence has this decline come? Some would say that it is due to the two wars, to the general unsettlement, to the influence of modern life, to quick and easy transport, to the cinema, the radio, to anything else in that kind that you care to think of. Some would lay it at the door of an educational system which they would say produces the educationally half-baked. Some would quite simply ascribe it to the Devil. Others would say that in Scotland we are only seeing a part of the general decline in authority and power of attraction which the Protestant Churches are suffering from all over Christendom as a result of their attempts to water down the mysteries of Faith, to meet the man in the street half way. They would point out that it is a general experience that whenever the guardians of these mysteries step forward to effect this half-way meeting the man in the street is inclined to step back the same distance and is even thus further from the church door.

> Loud mockers in the roaring street
> Say Christ is crucified again;
> Twice pierced His gospel-bearing feet,
> Twice broken His great heart in vain.

'You will not,' say these critics, 'encourage the ordinary man to defend Christ from these modern mockers by making it easy for him to compromise with their mockery. The stridency of their voices will soon overcome your sweet reasonableness. Cling rather to the assertion of the mystery of your Faith, and there you will find your answer. "*Credo quia impossibile est*" they might add, "is in its modern use usually either an exhausted evasion of effort or a cynical wisecrack. But *Credo quia possibile sit* is no better. It is even weaker; for who has yet been moved to passionate Faith by the thought that something may be possible"?' 'One thing is certain' they will conclude, 'when the Ministers of the Presbyterian Church in Scotland preached the mystery of their Faith four square direct and without compromise from that Book which they believed to contain the Revealed Word of God, their churches were fuller, their words more listened to than to-day, and their authority greater.'

The Church in Scotland is endeavouring to meet its modern difficulties in a number of ways. The Iona Community with its monastic discipline, its insistence on the Columban origin of the Church, undoubtedly provides a religious stimulus for a certain number of the younger members, but their number is not large. The movement is in some ways similar to the Anglo-Catholic revival in England, though the comparison is a dangerous one. There is, as a result partly of the St Columbans and partly of individual effort, some noble Church work being done in the slums and poorer parts of the great industrial cities. And in the country districts, unobserved and uncommented upon by the outside world, the personal sanctity of many an old-fashioned parish minister is doing more to preserve and further his Church's reputation than many an eminent Church statesman.

But if there is within the Church a vital spirit that is at once new and traditional it is to be found in those younger and young middle-aged ministers who have returned from the second World War with a determination to evangelize Scotland according to the message of the New Testament. These men are as much in reaction from the enervating 'modern moderatism' which between the wars sought to compromise with the modern unbeliever as were the moderates themselves in reaction from the Old Testament preachers of the Word of God in the last century. It has been said that the ministers of our grandfathers' and great-grandfathers' time spoke and preached and even looked like Old Testament prophets, and that these their posterity seek to preach and work, even if they do not always succeed in looking, like Apostles. It may be that they will be able to spread the fire of their undoubted enthusiasm, or they may fail. But it is only through some such spirit that the dormant quality that inflamed the Protestant Reformed Church of Scotland over a hundred years ago at the time of the Disruption can be revived.

Of the remaining Presbyterians outside the Church of Scotland the only branch that carries any weight is the Free Church, which holds its annual Assembly at the same time as the Assembly of the Church of Scotland. These Presbyterians are the most rigid and conservative of their Faith who remain. They preach from the Old Testament in the old style and disapprove of nearly every manifestation of modern life. They are the twentieth-century representatives of the type immortalized under the name of David Deans by Scott in his novel *The Heart of Midlothian*. They are confined mostly to the remoter Highland and Island districts, and where they are in the majority they have succeeded in deflecting the passionate Celtic spirit into a passionate form of Puritanism. It is possible to smile at the obdurate remoteness they preserve in their manner of life and thought. It is possible to feel strongly repelled by their luxury of disapproval. It is impossible, however, to withhold from them a certain admiration for their resolution and their dignity. They do at least believe.

There is one other highly respectable and long founded religious congregation that has come out of Scotland.

This is the Episcopalian Church in Scotland, which is in direct descent from the Episcopal body that was ousted from its official position and all but suppressed when the Church of Scotland was finally founded as a State Church in 1690. In the eyes of the average town-dwelling Scot the 'Piscies' are a small socially superior body who because they are in communion with the Church of England are a kind of social and religious Quislings. In the country places the Episcopal Church is often regarded as the place where the laird's friends who are up from England for the shooting repair to perform their social and religious duties by 'going to church'. Though one can understand the origin of that point of view it is unjust. The Scottish Episcopalians are Scottish in origin and strongly Scottish in sympathy. Two hundred years ago they suffered as a religious body more actively than did any other from the persecution following upon the 1745 rising. Possibly the only true believing, one might almost say practising, Jacobites left in Scotland are to be found in their Communion. The Scottish Episcopalians are, of course, touched and influenced by their connexion (it is no more than a connexion) with the Anglican Church, and when they are so influenced they tend to be 'Broad' and 'Moderate'. When, as in Aberdeenshire (and in other places where they are traditionally strong), they suck their sustenance from purely Scottish circumstances and Scottish air, they characteristically and nationally run to one of two extremes. They are either so simple in their forms of religious ceremony that they verge upon the practice of Presbyterianism or they are extremely ritualistic. Your real High Church Scottish Episcopalian is said to be 'higher than the Pope of Rome'. He is certainly 'higher' than the average Scottish Roman Catholic.

The average decent Scotsman at the beginning of the nineteenth century would have been startled and horrified if he had known that in a hundred and fifty years the Catholics in Scotland would amount in number to nearly half the official membership of the Church of Scotland. To-day these figures pass without much comment or complaint except in some urban circles which are actuated more by the fever of political bigotry than by religious fervour.

The remarkable increase in the number of Catholics in Scotland through the nineteenth century was largely the result of the Irish immigration; and to-day in Glasgow and the Western industrial districts the Catholic population has a predominant Irish flavour – at least as far as names are a guide. At first the presence of impoverished Irish Catholics in the growing and enrichening city of Glasgow stirred up strong anti-Catholic as well as racial strife. The vexed question of 'the Irish in Glasgow' has been discussed at some length in an earlier chapter. It only remains here to say that, while the racial problem is far from settled, purely religious anti-Catholic feeling has, to the credit of all parties, largely died down.

There remains, however, a tendency in certain circles to describe the Catholic Church in Scotland as an Irish Mission. Those who speak thus do so without a knowledge of the facts. The traditional body of native-born Scottish Catholics which survived the persecutions of the seventeenth and eighteenth centuries, and which incidentally was responsible for the establishment of the first Catholic churches in Glasgow since the Reformation, remains the hard core of Catholicism in Scotland. Rome has recognized this fact in appointing the majority of the Scottish hierarchy, since its re-establishment, from native

Scottish Catholic circles. This is not to say that there does not exist a certain 'watchfulness' of each other between the Irish and the traditional Scottish Catholics. In 1878 when the first Catholic Bishop of Glasgow was appointed since the Reformation that 'watchfulness' might have developed into something that would have deserved a stronger word. In this book there have been occasional strictures passed upon our amiable but somewhat heavy-footed Southern neighbours the English. It is pleasant in a chapter devoted to religion to record that it was the statesmanlike rule of the saintly Archbishop George Eyre, who was the first to fill the Catholic episcopal throne in Glasgow since Queen Mary, which was responsible for bringing about harmony between the Scots and Irish Catholics – he was an Englishman.

This is not the place to describe the severity and rigour of the oppression and persecution which the traditional Scottish Catholics had to endure for nearly two hundred and fifty years after the Reformation. Nor would it be proper for this pen, which is wielded by an adherent of the 'Old Religion', to write such a description. Let it be enough to say that it would startle some of our compatriots who sometimes seem to think that having been persecuted in the past for one's Faith is a prerogative of Covenanters and Presbyterians.

The fact that any native Scottish Catholics as a body survived these two hundred and fifty years was due to the fortitude of their Faith, and, to be fair, to the knowledge of support from far abroad – though this support was more of psychological than of practical value. Their survival was also due to the fact that the Catholic Faith was during this period the most ardently held in the remoter parts of the Highlands and Islands and in certain parts of tenacious Aberdeenshire, where it was difficult, for a number of reasons, for oppression to be more than sporadic – though when it did occur it was as savage as elsewhere.

The result is that there exist to-day in parts of Scotland quite substantial communities of Catholics who have never lost their Faith from before the Reformation. With the exception of a few courageous and much smaller communities in the North of England these are the only survivals in this kind in the United Kingdom. They are to be found in the Barra Islands, in South Uist, and in Canna in the Hebrides. On the mainland they exist in strength in that comparatively large district known to Scottish Catholics as Holy Morar. There are also pockets of them in remoter Aberdeenshire. They are of a peculiar sweetness of disposition and they practise their Faith easily and simply, like children, and as if they had never been persecuted nor were now, as far as their position in the country is concerned, isolated. In many things they are an example to Catholics all over the world.

It is a grateful task to end this long chapter so largely devoted to the telling of the story of so much bitterness, hatred, and dispute engendered in the name of religion in Scotland by paying a tribute to the relationship that exists between these remote Catholics and their Presbyterian neighbours around their districts. It is one of true harmony of a kind rarely if ever to be found existing between Protestants and Catholics living next door to each other. It is a harmony that is positive, for it does not recline upon indifference, but rests rather upon the strength of Faith which each recognizes in the other. These Highland and Scottish Catholics, these Highland Scottish Presbyterians are in this matter an example to all Christendom.

CHAPTER NINE

THE NEW NATIONALISM

Cultural and Political

EARLY in the 1930's Hugh MacDiarmid wrote these lines :

> The rose of all the world is not for me.
> I want for my part
> Only the little white rose of Scotland
> That smells sweet and breaks the heart.

They were struck out of the poet's imagination by a phrase used in conversation by Compton Mackenzie, and later (after the publication of the poem) introduced by Mackenzie into his address to the students when he was elected first Scottish Nationalist Lord Rector of Glasgow University. The poem was the product not only of MacDiarmid's political nationalism, the cause of which he was then, as he is now, ardently pursuing, but of a deeper feeling which he as a poet had been intermittently expressing for a number of years. These lines of his, though they are well known in Scotland, are not regarded by his more esoteric admirers as amongst his best – for they are written in English – but they do succeed in expressing both poignantly and popularly the feeling which has animated that movement, sometimes unfortunately and pompously described as 'The Scottish Renaissance in Literature and the Arts'.

This movement came into being as a result of a spark which ignited a certain amount of readily combustible material which in Scotland was waiting to be touched off

soon after the first World War. The spark was the publication of the early poetry of C. M. Grieve, who wrote,
and still writes when he is in a passionate mood, over the
name of Hugh MacDiarmid. The combustible material
was in the minds of a number of young men who had
returned from a war in defence of small nations, to find
their own small nation of Scotland in their view supinely
and decadently allowing itself to lose its individuality in
what seemed to them the amorphous conception of Great
Britain. Such material was ready to be ignited.

Ignited is not too strong a word for what happened; for
while there have been no bright crackling flames as a
result of those Shelleyean sparks of MacDiarmid's the
mass of material which was touched by them has continued obstinately to glow and give out a small but steady
heat like a banked-up peat fire in the innermost room of a
house. Such a fire does not make much light, nor, though
it be placed at the heart of the house, does it centrally
heat, in the modern sense of that phrase, the whole
building. You have to seek it out from room to room if
you wish to feel its warmth, and to look deeply into it if
you are to see the crimson and the gold and the white
rose of its deep incandescence.

'I want for my part only the little white rose of Scotland.' It was in some such mood that the writers and
speakers and dreamers in the Scotland who emerged in
the 1920's began to try and express themselves about their
native country to which they had returned. Their mood
was urgent; for they felt that things in Scotland were bad,
that she had already gone far along the road that would
lead in the end to the loss of her individuality, to the
disappearance of one of the most ancient nations in
Europe – their own nation. They looked across the Irish

Sea and saluted the burning spirit which had animated the Irish revival not only in politics but in the use of words and ideas. They could almost find it in their hearts to wish that Scotland had suffered an oppression of the kind from which the Irish had just freed themselves; for they recognized that their own country's individuality was all the more dangerously threatened by the insidiousness of the attack upon it – partly from within and partly by peaceful absorption from without.

They felt their mood to be urgent; and if they did not all have talents, let alone the genius, suitable to that mood, they were themselves urgent – urgent enough to provoke comment, sardonic, approving, or frankly hostile, from all over the country.

The sardonic comments were of the kind that Scotsmen of a particular cast of mind are so adept at producing when they detect enthusiasm in their midst. (The remarks of Lord Braxfield, whose appalling comment on the greatest example of 'giving oneself away' in all history, quoted in an earlier chapter, may be recalled, would have been interesting if he had been alive at the time.) But sardonic comments have never seriously wounded anyone used to life in Scotland: we are too accustomed to them.

Nor did the hostility which the movement aroused have much dampening effect. This hostility was based partly on political grounds (Ireland was considered a dangerous example then – though not so dangerous now) and partly on an anger aroused by the iconoclasm of the younger men in the movement who had little respect for the literary and artistic Scottish gods of their fathers' and grandfathers' time. They were particularly scathing at the expense of those Scottish authors such as J. M. Barrie and Ian Maclaren and the 'Kailyarders' who in their view

had sentimentalized and prostituted Scottish talent fo
the English market. Even poor Stevenson came in fo
some undeserved buffets on this score. The main them
of this hostility was that all this talk about a Scottisl
artistic and national revival was a temporary and irritat
ing phase which would pass over in a year or so. The
were mistaken. The so-called Scottish Renaissance, whicl
was eagerly seized upon by the journalists in this country
as a stunt well worth writing up for a short while, has ob
stinately remained 'news' for a quarter of a century.

The main desire of those who worked in this literary
revival was to build the new writing in their country upon
the foundations of an older Scotland which had not been,
as they saw it, by Anglicizing influences. They claimed
that the Scottish genius expressed itself to its best advantage in one of the Scottish languages or at least in the
Scottish idiom, and that it became weakened and untrue
to itself when Scotsmen tried to force themselves into the
foreign English mode of writing and thought. Fantastic
though this may still seem to-day, and absurd though the
'North Britons' in Scotland said it was at the time, these
Scottish literary revivalists were able to produce some
arguable proofs of their contention from the past. They
pointed out that Walter Scott was never so powerful as
when he was speaking through the mouths of his Scottish
characters in the Scottish tongue, never so ineffectual as
when he was expressing lofty English sentiments in high
English. They claimed and with some justification that
Stevenson in his Scots prose and poems was natural,
direct, unaffected, and never displayed those faults and
mannerisms which creep into his English work. The more
reasonable of them did not decry this English work, but
added that the Stevenson who in the end reverted to his

rue self in creating *Weir of Hermiston* would have been a greater writer if he had never left that true self.

They produced a number of other instances of this kind; but their trump card was, of course, Robert Burns. This outstanding and purely native poetic genius of Scotland wrote in the Scots tongue without modification, false refinement or corruption, at a time when that tongue was in literary circles at its depth of unpopularity. At the end of the eighteenth century, when Burns was struggling against the difficulties of humble origin and simple education for the mere recognition of his talents, let alone for fame, all influential Scotland was abasing itself before English manners, and seeking, often with a ludicrous and usually with an enfeebling effect, to write in the English language. Yet it was at this time and in these circumstances that Burns, seemingly impelled by a force outside himself, used the Scottish language to express himself, and, through himself, the heart of Scotland. No one has in pure poetry done it better. Even the refinement-loving, Anglican-leaning literary Scotland of his time recognized him for what he was. Even to-day he remains in his own kind and in what he did pre-eminent. Even to-day his fame is European, international, and not merely British or Scottish.

And it was this last fact that was often and triumphantly put forward in support of their beliefs by the adherents of the new Scottish literary movement. It was a favourite point of attack against them that they were, in their literary and artistic dreams, indulging in a kind of neo-provincialism, an escape into an artistic backwater cut off from the main stream of life. They would deny this by saying that, though it was provincial to write in dialect with the condescending knowledge that one was using a humble means of expression, and even more provincial to ape a foreign or metropolitan way of writing and speaking and thinking without succeeding, it was not provincial to use your own national tongue that had been natural to your nation however obscure and remote. It was, in short, not provincial to write in Scots like Robert Burns from the little country of Scotland upon the fringes of Northern Europe, and be translated into nearly every European tongue, but it was provincial to try and write like someone else, to write like a North Briton trying to write like a South Briton.

Inspired by these beliefs they looked back, and perforce deeply back into the Scottish past for the sources from which they could draw for their avowed purpose of expressing themselves in their own language. In that past there were two such sources, both ancient and traditional, yet both alive and still contributing to the stream of life if not of literature in the country. That these sources were no longer contributing to the literature of Scotland was not, it was claimed, because they had grown feeble or were unworthy, but because they had been quite deliberately prevented from doing so, had been, in fact, deflected from the main stream by the false Anglicization of Scottish letters. These two sources were, of course, the Gaelic and the traditional Lowland Scots language. It may be imagined with what gusto young, eager, poetically minded young Scots, with all their native passion for learning, turned to the delightful task of rescuing and using these oppressed, but far from suppressed, national languages.

It was easy at the time to smile at an enthusiasm of this kind engendered between poetry, learning, and nationalism. Some did more than smile, they derided it as false and foolish affectation. That this was unjust was shown, as some of us would maintain, by future events; but even before these events it would be shown that there was reason as well as feeling in these enthusiasms.

Scottish Gaelic is a noble and expressive language of high distinction and ancient lineage. At one time it was the language of the whole, and two hundred years ago of half of Scotland. It is still in the blood of most of us and on the tongues of a distinguished minority of speakers and writers who have always taken a proud delight in expressing themselves in it. It never retreated in Scotland to the extent that its twin sister, the Irish Gaelic, did in Ireland. Indeed, to encourage it, to strengthen its position, to work for its revival in literature in Scotland was a less deliberately self-conscious action than to do the same for Erse across the Irish Sea.

Lowland Scots was different. In some ways its use as a literary language was easier, in other ways more difficult. It certainly aroused greater opposition. It certainly provided an ample field for controversy. Here was a language which had been spoken at the Court of Stewart Kings, which had been the vehicle for the poetry of Dunbar and Henryson in the fifteenth and sixteenth centuries. In polite literary usage it had declined for the next two hundred years; yet it had obstinately remained the everyday speech not only of peasants and of poor people, but of all Lowland Scotland, of nobles and judges as well as of men of business in the cities, until the middle of the eighteenth century. Then when it might have been expected that it would retreat altogether from literature, there came Robert Burns, who used the Scottish language to become an internationally famous poet. Finally, the fact remains that to-day throughout rural Lowland Scotland and, to a lesser extent in the poorer parts of the cities, the language persists vigorously alive, not only in the hearts but on the lips of the people.

All this was true, but it served at first only to complicate the issue. To convince people that Scots was a proper means of literary expression in the twentieth century was a formidable task. If you went back to Henryson or Dunbar for your proofs or for the source of the language you used you were accused of an affected archaism. If you sought your inspiration from Burns you were told that you were singeing your wings at the flame of a unique genius. And if you turned to contemporary Scots speech as spoken in the Borders, in Aberdeenshire, on the middle east coast or in Galloway, you aroused a different kind of hostility. You offended the entire Scots middle, or rising middle, class, the members of which had spent the most important part of their socially rising years in laboriously trying to get rid of the taint of the Scots language either in word, idiom, or accent.

Nevertheless it was in the language of Lowland Scotland which those who believed in the Scottish Renaissance most eagerly, most effectively, and most controversially tried to say what they had to say. They claimed that they got over the difficulty of there being no one accepted standard for living Lowland Scots, which varies in the pronunciation, spelling, and sometimes in the meaning of words according to districts, by quite deliberately setting a standard of their own. This standard they made by choosing the most generally accepted words from the living language as spoken to-day and (particularly in verse) by strengthening and lending colour to their use of this living language by reviving certain words from the Middle Scots period of Dunbar and Henryson. In the exuberance of poetic scholarship they would sometimes introduce verbal concepts of their own made by the blending of French, German, or Latin words with their Scottish near counterparts. When laughed at for this occasional tendency they would point out that this was exactly what the old poets used to do in both Scots and English when the languages were growing. Why should they not do the same now that they were, in poetry at least, encouraging the re-growth of a language? And sometimes (though it must be added that this was only done as a kind of joke) they would invent Scottish phrases for new things which did not have natural names in Scots. The most grotesque examples of this were 'faur-speke' for telephone, and (an invention of the present writer's) 'ootlands screiver' for Foreign Secretary.

At this point the earnest reader from abroad may well lay down this book and ask whether he is being invited to consider as if they were serious the pranks of some high-spirited undergraduates and the conceits of a few middle-aged eccentrics. And certainly in Scotland itself there have not been wanting critics who with increasing irritation and even anger have dismissed the whole of the new school in Scottish poetry and writing in these terms. Despite this, however, the new school has now for twenty-five years gone on producing with varying success verse and plays, but seldom prose, in this language which Professor Denis Saurat sympathetically described as 'synthetic Scots', which its opponents call 'plastic Scots' and which has recently reacquired the pleasant sounding and traditional name of Lallans, used by both Burns and Stevenson – meaning the Lowland, as apart from the Highland (Heilan) tongue of Scotland. The reacquisition, the partly humorous use of this old Scots word has, for some reason, particularly infuriated the more old fashioned type of critic who represents in his or her writing the apogee of middle-class, self-conscious literary rectitude in Scotland.

Despite all this, despite the difficulties that face any new school of enthusiasts, despite their sometimes humorous, and sometimes, it must be admitted, humourless, pedantry, these writers have achieved something noteworthy, if only in being the continual subject of discussion in intelligent circles in Scotland for a quarter of a century. They would, however, deny that they write only for the esoteric. They claim that any Scot brought up in Scotland who approaches their work sympathetically can understand and feel what they are saying. They insist that they are strengthening a language still alive and potent and not reviving a moribund one. They can produce one or two practical proofs in support of this claim.

Shortly after the last war the Citizens' Theatre in Glasgow (the Scottish Repertory company founded by James Bridie) put on *Jamie the Saxt* by Robert McLellan. McLellan is a playwright of experience who has chosen to write in the Scots tongue. This play, the scene of which was placed at the Court of James VI of Scotland and I of England in Edinburgh just before James's accession to the English throne, was, with the exception of the part of the English Ambassador from Queen Elizabeth, written and played entirely in Scots without any attempt to water it down or make it easy. There was obviously historical and dramatic justification for this, but a number of critics who saw the play in rehearsal wondered whether any but a few scholars would understand it. In fact, *Jamie the Saxt* played to crowded audiences of the ordinary Scottish kind for a number of weeks in Glasgow, Perth, and Ayr. It could be revived successfully at any time in Lowland Scotland to-day. If it were to be produced in London it would be naturally only a curiosity; for no one could blame the ordinary audience there for finding it incomprehensible. Even the most sympathetic English visitors who can read the play in print were, when they saw it in Scotland, largely defeated by the sound of spoken Scots. The fact that this same spoken Scots of a rather learned kind was enjoyed by a variety of audiences in Scotland was proof that at least one 'Lallans writer' has reached the ordinary public ear in this country.

There was another and smaller incident which with more pathos made a similar point. A Scottish writer who was speaking in support of a Scottish Nationalist political candidate at a rural district in the East Lowlands found himself at an informal meeting of farmers and small town business men. They asked him whether all this revival of the Scottish language was not 'so much nonsense', and whether anything that he had written in this kind could really be understood by them – plain ordinary Scots folk. For an answer this rather peculiar-looking literary man, black-bearded and immensely elongated, drew himself up to his full six and a half feet and recited to them his own translation of the Twenty-Third Psalm in Scots. When he had finished there was a long silence; and the present writer can vouch for it that one or two of these practical East Coast Lowland farmers were near to tears. What had seized them was the unexpectedness of it all. Here was that Psalm which possibly above all other parts of the Bible had been most familiar and dear to them since childhood spoken to them not in the conventional tongue to which they had been accustomed in Church but in the language of their childhood and of their hearts. It was, in a sense, the first time they had ever heard, truly heard, the Twenty-Third Psalm.

Some of the poetry of Hugh MacDiarmid, the founder and inspirer of the movement, has also reached the public ear and has gone beyond more than literary circles. He is a poet of distinction, and his verses had at one time the authentic sudden lyric beauty which allows them to be compared with Burns' poetry. He has won international recognition, as well as fame in his own country, that is to say in Ireland (Yeats was a strong admirer of his), in America, on the Continent, and in England. Under his own name of C. M. Grieve (he is a Border Scot) he is a lively, controversial, if somewhat ungrammatical, polemical writer in prose. However much one may agree with or be irritated by his views and his way of expressing them, he is always worth listening to. In appearance, or rather in the impression that the appearance his shock-headed, frail, ethereal little body presents, he reminds one of a mixture between a thistle and Shelley, an improbable combination which one has to see to believe.

He has had his followers and imitators amongst the younger men, the more successful of whom include Sidney Goodsir Smith (again an undeniably authentic poet who has been most generously praised in England as well as at home). But though they are urgent and have, some of them, strong poetic talent as well as feeling, none has as yet touched the level reached by MacDiarmid's verses. One cannot leave the subject of living Scottish poetry without mentioning the name of Lewis Spence. This scholarly veteran was fighting the battle for the recognition of Scottish verse (and was writing it too) at the turn of the century. But he is, strictly speaking, outside the movement.

Hovering on the edge of this poetic circle, most power-fully influencing it, as he influences so much else in Nationalist circles in Scotland, is the same tall bearded figure already referred to of that remarkable scholar, Douglas Young, at once the Don Quixote and the modern Sir Thomas Urquhart of the Scottish movement to-day.

That movement, though in a literary sense its origin was in poetry, is not confined to poets. Prose writers in fiction, in the drama, in journalism both literary and popular, have been attracted to and influenced by it and in varying degrees and at varying removes try to express its inspiration. The names of a number of these mean much to us in Scotland, some to the outside world. Amongst these are those of Neil Gunn, the late James Bridie, and Eric Linklater. Gunn is a passionate suppor-ter. Bridie, though he allowed his sardonic but always kindly humour full play in satirizing modern Scotland, was clearly influenced by the *motif* of modern Scottish letters, and was always ready to join battle in defence of the new Scottish literature. Linklater might hesitate to align himself with this or any movement, but that it con-tinually occupies his thoughts and touches his writing cannot be denied. Finally, like a comet with a multi-coloured tail, Compton Mackenzie flashed across our sky in the 1920's and 30's until his health drove him South again. He never attempted verse or prose in the Scots language, but his generous and whole-hearted interest in the movement did much to encourage and actively help younger writers in it. He has written much about the New Scotland, in essays, historical studies, and, let it be added, in satire, but the most intimate revelation of his thoughts on the subject are contained in his novel *The North Wind of Love*.

One could go on adding names which might or might not mean anything to the reader, but it is more fitting to end one's attempt to answer the question of what the 'Scottish Renaissance in Literature and Art' has achieved by saying one thing – and it is for one whose business and preoccupation it is to live and work and write in the Scotland of to-day a more eloquent answer than the longest list of names, books, and plays – it is this. For the last twenty years in this small country of ours the writer of poems, plays, fiction, essays, political polemics, or contemporary journalism (and in a more restricted way this is true of the other arts) has been able to feel that he has had a theme worth writing about which is both outside himself and larger than himself, and yet is intensely personal to himself. That theme is Scotland.

It would be too much to say that in Edinburgh, Glasgow, Aberdeen, Dundee, Inverness, Perth, all rolled into one, we have achieved what must have been the artistic atmosphere of Dublin at the end of last century and at the beginning of this one. It would be too much to say that we have produced our Yeats, our Synge, or our Sean O'Casey yet (though we have had some near misses), but we do know that we have enjoyed something of the exultation which these and other Irishmen must have felt in the creative impulse of an art which came from their own country as well as from themselves.

In national revivals literature and politics usually go together. And so nearly all those who wrote under the influence of the new movement or who were attracted by it were professed Scottish nationalists; though by no means all political nationalists comprehended or approved by their artistic allies. Indeed, some of them may well have been embarrassed by the decorative excesses in appearance and in words of these supporters. At the beginning the political movement suffered from the reputation of being run by poets, novelists, and cranks. Looking back at this distance and from a time when no one could bring such an accusation one can comment that it is not at all unusual for new political movements to be conceived in the minds of 'men of the word', of artists and of what the world looks upon as peculiar people. Moreover, had it not been for the persistent publicity which these 'poets, novelists, and cranks' gave to the cause of Scottish nationalism in their writings and speeches that cause would not have been so constantly kept before Scotland, as it undoubtedly was in the years between the wars. One cannot help smiling when one hears to-day a hard-headed Scottish business man uttering nationalist sentiments which in the 1920's would have been dismissed by many as typical of the 'sentimental tosh talked by artistic nationalists'.

The political Nationalist movement of to-day began in 1928 when the National Party of Scotland was founded (characteristically enough) by a Glasgow University student, a poet, a lawyer, and a Gaelic-speaking aristocrat. These four men soon attracted some 10,000 members and more or less organized 100 branches. Political candidates were sporadically put forward by this party at elections until the present time. These candidates frequently lost their deposits; and only one of them, early in 1945, succeeded in being elected to the Westminster Parliament. This state of affairs has puzzled even the most sympathetic observers who ask how it is that (though they never heard of Scottish nationalism outside Scotland) whenever they came to the country in the 1930's they found it a continual subject of dispute. It particularly puzzles them to-day when the 'Scottish Covenant' demanding a Scottish Parliament for Scottish affairs bears just over two million signatures. To offer any kind of an answer it is necessary briefly to put forward an account of the political national feeling in Scotland since the Union of Parliaments.

After this Union, 1707, and until half-way through the eighteenth century there was a fairly widespread feeling throughout the country of national frustration and dissatisfaction at the loss of Scotland's political individuality. This dissatisfaction declined almost to disappearing point as a result of the prosperity that came with the opening of trade with the Western world, the agricultural revolution, and finally the Industrial Revolution. Throughout the nineteenth century it cannot be said that Scots were entirely easy that their affairs were being properly and sympathetically managed at Westminster, but they consoled themselves with the thought that their countrymen often occupied such high positions in the Government at London. There was also born then the flattering notion that wherever you went in the British Empire you always found a Scot who was 'heid o' a depairtment'. This was the century in which Scots recompensed themselves for what they believed to be the now final disappearance of their country as a political entity by a strident assertion of their 'Scotchness' in other things. This was the mark of provincial rather than national feeling.

Nevertheless, the rise of the radical wing of the Liberal Party in the 1880's and the Irish Home Rule movement at the same time did bring about a Scottish Home Rule movement in the House of Commons. This movement is now almost forgotten, but that it was not negligible is shown by the fact that of the five attempts made in the last decade of the century to move a Home Rule motion four were supported by a majority of Scottish members. In this century the Liberals under Asquith revived the idea of Federal Home Rule, and in 1913 Sir W. H. Cowan's Scottish Home Rule Bill actually passed its second reading by 204 votes to 159 (Scots 45 to 8). The 1914 War, however, in defence of Serbia and Belgium, obliterated the chances of this quiet but important move in favour of a nearer small nation.

After the 1914 War nothing was heard of Home Rule until the formation of the National Party in 1928. That the movement thus started or rather revived had an immediate and disseminated effect in all parts of Scotland cannot be denied. Indeed, the attacks upon it, based either on ridicule or other propaganda, paid unwilling tribute to this. The Lowlanders were told that this was a sentimental Celtic Highland ramp; the Highlanders were warned that it was an attempt by the Lowlanders to gain control of Scotland; Glasgow was informed that this was Edinburgh's last effort to bolster up her decadent position as a capital; Edinburgh was asked to fight it as emanating from the 'Red Clyde'. And of course religion entered into it. The Scottish Home Rule movement was either a Roman Catholic or an extreme Protestant plot according to the audience that you were addressing. The truth was that Home Rule for Scotland had supporters more or less equally distributed in all these quarters.

This in a sense was its weakness from the point of view of the practicalities of the game of party politics. In every constituency there was a minority of workers for Home Rule, desperately in earnest, always vocal and sometimes talented. It was a classless minority (one of its leaders was a Duke, another was a miner) which kept the matter constantly in people's minds in Scotland and which in between election times was able to convince a number of waverers in each constituency of the justice of their claims. When the fever of election time came round, however, these waverers not unnaturally forgot everything else in the urgency of turning Mr Baldwin or Mr Churchill or Mr Attlee out or keeping them in. The Home Rule party then which continued, to the irritation of its opponents, to remain news continued also, with one exception in Motherwell in 1945, to lose every election for which it put up candidates. It is easy now to say that it was mistaken tactics for them to try and fight their cause according to conventions of party politics, but it is difficult to see what else they could have done. At least they kept the matter obstinately alive.

After the second World War the position was completely and dramatically changed by what is loosely known as 'the Covenant Movement'. Very briefly what happened was this: Scottish Convention, a non-party body drawn from all walks of life in Scotland, put forward to the Labour Secretary of State for Scotland, Mr Arthur Woodburn, proposals in favour of a 'sub-parliament' for Scotland. Mr Woodburn said that he thought them reasonable but denied that there was any public support for them. To prove its point then Scottish Convention, through a National Assembly which it called in 1949, issued to the public a covenant pledging the signatories to do everything in their power to support a Parliament in Scotland for Scottish affairs within the framework of the United Kingdom and in full loyalty to the Throne. Within six months the covenant had acquired a million signatures. At the time of writing the figure is two million – over half the voting population of Scotland.

The covenant was cautiously supported by the majority of the Scottish Press, but was, of course, violently attacked in certain quarters, particularly in the *Glasgow Herald*, the last organ of pure Whiggery in the country. The attackers mainly confined themselves to pointing out that, whatever care the organization took, there was no absolute guarantee that people had not signed twice or three times. They added that many signatories did not properly appreciate what they were signing, or might have been drunk when they signed! And so on. Making all due allowances for these arguments which cannot be disproved they ceased to have much validity when the two million mark was passed, for even if one allows that half those who signed were dishonest or incompetent for one of these reasons, the residue of a million Scots is not negligible.

There at present the matter rests. Neither the Government nor the Opposition have agreed, on the strength of these remarkable figures, to the proposal of a plebiscite; but it is clear that both sides are trying to gain the support of a movement which they now find was bigger than they had expected. At the time of writing it is uncertain whether the organizers of the covenant will enter the political field or will concentrate on using their valuable non-party status to make propaganda outside as well as in Scotland. Whatever they do, and whatever mistakes they may make, they have, however, now started something that has acquired a large momentum of its own.

It would be dishonest (even if he could effectively do so after what he has already said here) for the present

writer to disguise his sympathies and hopes for the Home
Rule Movement in Scotland and his pleasure in the success of the covenant up to date. At the same time he does
not feel himself so passionately involved as to be debarred
from the right to try and present an objective comment on
the state of affairs in this matter as they are at present –
not as they may be in the future, but now at the time of
writing.

That about half the adult population of Scotland is in
varying degrees unhappy about the position of their
country in the United Kingdom is difficult to deny.
Those who feel thus are drawn from all ranks in the
Right and in the Left, but they are far from being united
on the means to put matters right. Opinion varies from
that held by the small body of extremists who would not
be content even with Dominion status but who demand
a cut as clean as that made by the Irish Republic, to
those who understandably recoil in horror from such a
suggestion but who feel that something must be done, and
done politically, to save Scotland not only for herself but
for the United Kingdom. The extremists we have always
had with us since the beginning of the movement. They
are vocal but numerically small; nor are they likely to
increase unless the flouting of public opinion is even more
tactlessly conducted by the Government than it has been
already. This point has often been put forward by the
balanced moderate opinion.

The majority of the large numbers of those who felt
sufficiently unhappy about Scotland's position to sign the
Covenant have no very clear idea of the form a Scottish
Parliament should take – something vaguely on the lines
of the Ulster model is as near as most people get. It is
perhaps one of the weaknesses of the Covenant Movement

that its leaders have not publicly attempted to give a shape to public opinion in this matter. But again this is questionable. It is not always wise to have things too cut and dried in advance. Another weakness of the movement is that news of it, even the two million signatures, has been largely confined to Scotland, and little attempt has been made to inform even the most generous and sympathetic of our generous sister nation that such a movement exists. It is this that gives such incidents as the removal of the Stone of Destiny from Westminster Abbey a publicity value disproportionate to their true significance.

Home Rule is, of course, most strongly opposed by a large number of people in Scotland – more strongly, more potently, and more vocally than in England. These vary from the extremists who, in their own way, are as fanatical as the extremists on the other side, to those who, with deep sincerity and patriotism, believe that the process of Union with England has gone too far to be reversed without grave damage to Scotland. There has been much argument between the more reasonable statisticians, economicians, and political philosophers on both sides on this point, but, it need hardly be said, without much effect. In any event, the opponents would conclude 'this is not the time to make such an experiment'. It should be stressed that these opponents include many who are sincere and fervent Scottish patriots as well as loyal citizens of Great Britain.

Reference in these pages has been made to that endemic Scottish failing, disunity, splitting up, 'hiving off', excessive individuality, however you like to call it. Scotland would not be Scotland were this tendency not already displaying itself in the Home Rule movement. And already small splinter parties in the old eighteenth-century religious tradition of the multiplication of sects have manifested themselves with their preposterous proposals and preposterous proclamation of individuality. The main movement has now reached proportions that no one could have suspected or hoped for twenty-five years ago. Its proportions are such that in the normal course of events it cannot now fizzle out; it cannot now be entirely ineffective. It would be asking too much of a large body of Scots people to expect them to get rid of a quality so radical in them as their excessive individualism, but if this tendency to disunity in the Home Rule movement is allowed to grow unchecked, the now inevitable effect of that movement will be delayed, weakened, impaired, and in the end made unworthy of the enthusiasm which conceived it.

There is another radical quality in the Scots. It is their self-respect; and from this self-respect comes the most valuable element in the movement for Scottish Home Rule, an element not usually to be found in a small nation struggling to re-assert itself. The Scottish movement is not built upon a sense of inferiority, upon fear or upon hate, but upon a desire for full self-respect. The average Scot does not feel inferior to the Englishman. He may fear the effect of the overwhelming numbers of the English and the absorbing and deadening effect upon national life of the centralization of affairs in the English Capital, but he does not fear the Englishman. And he certainly does not hate him. But he does wish to stand politically equal and level with the Englishman within the United Kingdom, for he believes that the long and proud history, the strong individuality of his nation warrants this. A large number of those who support Scottish Home Rule believe that this can come about only if

Scotland has control of her own affairs again. They believe that when this happens the true England will benefit as well as the true Scotland, and the Scottish people
will regain their full respect for themselves.

Hatred and fear, or the effects of these, often make
news. Other small nations who have been driven by
hatred and fear of their neighbours have found this to be
true and have used it in their propaganda to the world.
Self-respect or the desire for self-respect does not make
news. The supporters of the Scottish movement who
are well aware of and who understand the reasons for the
ignorance of their claims outside Scotland have, in their
experience of English politicians and publicists, found
this also to be true. Naturally they would wish this
ignorance did not exist, but they would scorn the suggestion that they should break it down by actions which
looked as if they were animated by hatred or fear of the
English, or of anyone else. They have too much self-
respect for that.

Postscript

No mention of the Border Towns. Aberdeen and Dundee only respectfully touched on in passing. The tradition of Scottish education ignored. The vast Hydro-Electric schemes for the reviving of Highland life only used in a sentence to illustrate an argument or provide an excuse for a pious hope. I know that these are only some of the more obvious omissions in this picture which I have tried to present of my countrymen and their country. I mention these omissions here not because I wish to apologize for them, but because I would not wish any reader to think that I was unaware of them.

I do not apologize for them because I have deliberately set out to present Scotland and the Scots as I see them and can only speak with feeling and knowledge on those aspects of them which I believe myself to know about, which have absorbed my deepest interests over a number of years. Were I with the aid of much reading and enquiry to have made myself write about other elements in Scottish life which, however important I know them to be, do not touch me in this way I think I should only have succeeded in passing on second hand knowledge; and if this study of Scotland to-day has any claims it is that it is one made at first hand.

There is only one omission which I personally regret: the Scottish dance. The traditional Scottish country dance (enjoyed quite as much in the towns as in the country) is one of the most truly popular of our pastimes, and it is as vigorously and unaffectedly national as any dance in Europe. It seems to me that, in its passionate formality, in its blending of abandon and style, in its rhythm of colour and pattern it expresses the Scottish spirit as almost nothing else does. Were I to be asked to *show* Scotland to a foreigner for one evening I would show him the Scottish dance. But how, alas! can it be shown in writing?

M. McL.

*The following pages
describe other recent
Penguin and Pelican
publications*

HIGHLAND DRESS

George F. Collie

K 46

The national dress of Scotland has for long fascinated both the Scot and the Sassenach, and the purpose of this King Penguin is to give a brief outline of its history and development and to reproduce a few of the beautiful plates from McIan's *The Clans of the Scottish Highlands* first published in 1845. There are twenty-four of these, reproduced in colour, showing the costume of as many different clans. (2s 6d)

ROBERT BURNS

H. W. Meikle and W. Beattie

D 3

This selection contains the majority of the best-known poems of Scotland's national poet, and includes a biography and explanatory notes on the language throughout the text. (1s 6d)

W. Beattie has also compiled an anthology of *Border Ballads* which will be published in the Penguin Poets series early in 1952.

THE IRISH

Sean O'Faolain

A 184

The story, told with detachment and criticism, of the development of Ireland, the character of its people and their contribution to civilization. It is divided into three parts, the old
Celtic World, the Christian Struggle and Downfall and
Uprise, and the author is equally at home with the old legends,
the learning of the Middle Ages and the recent political
troubles. (1s 6d)

SALOME AND OTHER PLAYS

Oscar Wilde

600

This volume contains *Salome*, *A Woman of No Importance* and *An
Ideal Husband*. *Salome*, with its odd moonlit beauty and the
luxuriance of its language, is more akin to a modern prose-poem
than to drama proper; while the other two are true Wildean
comedies, presenting serious themes in an easy, witty and fast-
moving style. (1s 6d)

The plays of another Irish playwright, J. M. Synge, will be
published shortly as a Penguin.

PRAY FOR THE WANDERER

Kate O'Brien

836

A successful writer returns to his home, a small town in Ireland,
in order to escape from the disturbing relationships of his
sophisticated life, but finds that living in Mellick is no more
restful. Kate O'Brien's accurate sense of place and period, and
of their exact social, political and religious atmosphere will be
expected by readers of *Mary Lavelle* (Penguin 801). (2s)

Wales

THE WELSH
Wyn Griffith
A215

'Within its compass *The Welsh* is easily the best available foreigner's guide to the understanding of the natives of Wales. The book is a mirror which should help not only the English to see the Welsh but the Welsh to see themselves.' – *Observer*

'Here is our history, our language, our literature, our arts (or lack of them), our poetry, our chapel-going and, to some extent, our politics, all explained with a lot of sound common sense.' – *Reynolds News*

A PROSPECT OF WALES
Gwyn Jones and Kenneth Rowntree
K43

'. . . a book of great beauty and scholarship containing some twenty-two reproductions of the water-colours of Kenneth Rowntree and a beautifully written essay by Gwyn Jones. His word-pictures of the beauties of Wales are a fitting prelude to the blaze of colour we meet in the later pages.' – *Manchester Evening News*. (2s 6d)

OFF TO PHILADELPHIA IN THE MORNING
Jack Jones
863

A novel of South Wales in the middle of the nineteenth century, portraying the people who toiled for a sparse living in the coal-pits yet preserved the traditions of their race and, above all, their passion for music. It is a biography within a novel, for the central figure is Joseph Parry the Welsh composer whose hymn-tune 'Aberystwyth' is the most famous of the hundreds he created, and Jack Jones has filled in the background with brilliant character sketches of the Welsh people. (3s 6d)

The Pelican History of England

While each volume is complete in itself, this whole series has been planned to provide an intelligent and consecutive guide to the development of English society in all its aspects. Of the eight volumes, five are already available.

TUDOR ENGLAND – *S. T. Bindoff, Professor of History at Queen Mary College, London*

ENGLAND IN THE EIGHTEENTH CENTURY – *J. H. Plumb, Fellow of Christ's College, Cambridge*

ENGLAND IN THE NINETEENTH CENTURY (1815–1914) – *David Thomson, Fellow of Sidney Sussex College, Cambridge*

THE BEGINNINGS OF ENGLISH SOCIETY (from the Anglo-Saxon Invasion) – *Dorothy Whitelock, Fellow of St Hilda's College, Oxford*

ENGLISH SOCIETY IN THE EARLY MIDDLE AGES 1066–1307 – *Doris Mary Stenton, Senior Lecturer at Reading University*

The others, which will follow as soon as possible, are:

ROMAN BRITAIN – *Professor Ian Richmond, King's College, Newcastle-on-Tyne*

ENGLAND IN THE LATE MIDDLE AGES – *A. R. Myers, Lecturer at Liverpool University*

ENGLAND IN THE SEVENTEENTH CENTURY – *Maurice Ashley, M.A.*

A New Penguin Series

THE BUILDINGS OF ENGLAND

Nikolaus Pevsner

Slade Professor of Fine Art at the University of Cambridge

This series is being launched to meet a growing demand from students and travellers for more detailed information about the history and architecture of the buildings they visit. It will provide a complete and authoritative introduction to the churches, monuments, and large houses, in fact to every structure of interest in a county from prehistoric remains to the latest building of note, treating them village by village and town by town, and in the case of churches describing not only the exterior but also the furnishings, such as pulpits, roof-bosses, plate and rood-screens. Each volume will contain a long general introduction to the architectural history of the county, a map, and a large section of illustrations.

The first three volumes, at three shillings and sixpence each, are:

CORNWALL, NOTTINGHAMSHIRE, MIDDLESEX

To follow early in 1952:

A volume on LONDON excluding the City and Westminster

NORTH DEVON

SOUTH DEVON

ATTITUDE TO AFRICA

W. Arthur Lewis, Michael Scott
Colin Legum and Martin Wight

s 159

This Penguin Special is a study of the present-day problems of British Africa. It is divided into four parts. The first is a survey of the general situation in Africa and the second treats of Britain's political responsibilities: while in the other two Michael Scott takes the particular case of the High Commission Territories of South Africa and discusses a policy of social development in the Bechuanaland Protectorate, and W. Arthur Lewis puts forward a programme for peasant agriculture. (2s)

THE AMERICAN UNION

H. G. Nicholas

A 207

A history of the United States, which is written in the conviction that the subject is of increasing interest to the British reader and that an introductory study which emphasizes the internal and distinctive features of American development may serve a useful purpose in explaining the United States of to-day.

THE ENGLISH PARLIAMENT

K. R. Mackenzie

A 208

A survey of the historical development of Parliament describing how and why it has come to work in the way it does to-day. *The Spectator* commented: 'Mr Mackenzie has done an altogether admirable piece of work, covering ground which has never been covered in so succinct a form, which badly needed to be covered and which is covered here as effectively as could be hoped for.'